Empower Your Child Guide to Thriving in Li

Are you grappling with the recent diagnosis of autism in your child, watching them navigate the challenges that come with the condition? Perhaps you're noticing signs of autism in your child, but haven't yet received a formal diagnosis, leaving you uncertain about the next steps.

Do you find yourself in need of a deeper understanding of autism and how to meet your child's unique needs? Are you struggling with the complexities of parenting a child on the autism spectrum?

Autism Spectrum Disorder (ASD) presents formidable challenges, pushing parents to their limits while also highlighting their strengths. This book is designed to accompany you on your journey, providing invaluable guidance as you navigate the complexities of parenting a child with autism.

Here's a glimpse of what you'll learn:

- **Discover what Autism Spectrum Disorder Is:** Learn what Autism Spectrum Disorder is, including what the term "spectrum" means.

- **The Power of Early Action:** Discover the power of early action, from recognizing the signs to navigating the diagnosis process.
- **Insights into Their Inner World:** Gain comprehensive insight into your child's inner world.
- **Fostering Growth and Development:** Understand how to create a foundation that bolsters your child's growth and development.
- **Connecting Through Nonverbal Communication:** Master the art of connecting to your child through nonverbal communication.
- **Crafting an Autism Management Plan:** Learn how to craft a customized autism management approach based on your child's needs and strengths.
- **Management Options for Autism Spectrum Disorder (ASD):** Explore different management options for ASD.
- **The Role of Self-Care:** Understand the role of self-care

while parenting a child on the autism spectrum.

- **Embracing the Unique Challenges:** Learn how to embrace the unique challenges and joy of raising a child with autism.

How to Help Your Child Thrive with Autism

A Parent's All You Need to Know Guide to Help Children with Autism Spectrum Disorder

Your Free Bonus

Scan the QR code below to claim your free Interactive Autism Workbook Mega Bundle & Autism Art Therapy Worksheets.

© **Copyright 2024 - All rights reserved.**

The content contained within this book may not be reproduced, duplicated, or transmitted without direct written permission from the author or the publisher.

Under no circumstances will any blame or legal responsibility be held against the publisher or author for any damages, reparation, or monetary loss due to the information contained within this book, either directly or indirectly.

Legal Notice:

This book is copyright-protected. It is only for personal use. You cannot amend, distribute, sell, use, quote, or paraphrase any part of the content within this book without the consent of the author or publisher.

Disclaimer Notice:

Please note the information contained within this document is for educational and entertainment purposes only. All effort has been executed to present accurate, up-to-date, reliable, and complete information. No warranties of any kind are declared or implied. Readers acknowledge that the author is not engaging in the rendering of legal, financial, medical, or professional advice. The content within this book has been derived from various sources. Please consult a licensed professional before attempting any techniques outlined in this book.

By reading this document, the reader agrees that under no circumstances is the author responsible for any losses, direct or indirect, that are incurred as a result of the use of the information contained within this document, including, but not limited to, errors, omissions, or inaccuracies.

Table of Contents

Introduction 1

Chapter 1: Decoding Autism 4

What Is Autism? Understanding the Spectrum 4

The Autism Spectrum 5

The Journey Ahead 7

Further Challenges, Hope and Triumphs ... 13

Debunking Myths 16

Key Takeaways 18

Chapter 2: The Power of Early Action .. 21

The Significance of Early Intervention 22

Monitoring Developmental Milestones 30

Navigating the Diagnosis Process 32

Stories for Inspiration 36

Key Themes across Success Stories 38

Key Themes across Impactful Cases 41

Key Takeaways 42

Chapter 3: Inside Your Child's World . 44

Building Understanding and Compassion 44

Behavior as Language 54

Developing Language Skills in Children with autism 57

Key Takeaways 60

Chapter 4: Creating a Foundation 63

Structuring a Home for Comfort and Growth 64

Significance of Routine in a Child with Autism's Life 73

Celebrating the Wins 75

Key Takeaways 80

Chapter 5: Beyond Words 82

Connecting through Nonverbal Communication 82

Key Takeaways 97

Chapter 6: Tailored Strategies............100

Creating a Customized Autism Management Plan 101

Tailored Strategies to Consider 107

Adapting the Plan 110

Key Takeaways 113

Chapter 7: Choosing the Path 116

A Spectrum of Therapies 116

Understanding Your Choices 125

A Holistic Approach 127

Key Takeaways 134

Chapter 8: The Caregiver's Journey...138

Self-Care for the Caregiver 143

Key Takeaways 153

Chapter 9: Educational Empowerment 156

Leveraging Special Education Services ...156

The Role of SIA in Social, Communication, and Behavior Improvement 158

Implementing Special Interests in the Child's Education 160

Key Takeaways 171

Chapter 10: Unique Challenges and Joys 174

Autism and Parenting 176

Empathy and Emotional Challenges 182

Dealing with Shame 185

Building a Support Network 187

Key Takeaways 191

Conclusion 193

References 196

Introduction

"Autism is not a disability, it's a different ability." - Stuart Duncan

Have you ever pondered what thoughts traverse the mind of a child with autism? Witnessing your child grapple with life's challenges and struggles to communicate can be an overwhelming experience for any parent. Naturally, you want to support them, yet you may find yourself unsure of where to begin or how to approach them without causing distress.

Rest assured, you are not alone in facing these dilemmas. Many parents of children with autism encounter similar obstacles. By delving into this book, you've taken the crucial first step toward comprehending your child's condition better and providing them with the assistance they require.

Let's embark on this journey together by delving into the intricacies of autism and gaining insight into its spectrum. Along the way, you'll learn to recognize the signs and symptoms of autism in children, enabling you to secure an early diagnosis and initiate effective symptom management.

Understanding the unique perspectives and preferences of children with autism can be challenging for parents. This book equips you with strategies to encourage your child to articulate their thoughts and feelings, fostering empathy and mutual understanding in the process.

Creating a nurturing environment within your home is essential for your child's well-being. You'll explore techniques for establishing a safe haven and implementing routines that promote growth and comfort.

Communication doesn't always rely on verbal language, especially for children with autism. You'll discover how to interpret their non-verbal cues and communicate with them effectively through gestures of affection and understanding.

Collaborating with healthcare professionals and devising tailored strategies are paramount in supporting your child's development. From exploring various management approaches to selecting appropriate therapies, you'll gain the tools to chart the most beneficial course for your child's unique needs.

Amidst the demands of caregiving, it's vital not to neglect your own well-being. This book underscores the importance of self-care and offers guidance on seeking support during challenging times.

Ensuring that educators and peers are informed about your child's condition is crucial for fostering inclusivity and understanding in educational settings. You'll learn advocacy strategies to safeguard your child's rights and ensure their needs are met within their learning environment.

Packed with case studies, insights, and actionable tips, this book serves as your companion in navigating the world of autism and devising effective management strategies for your child.

Let's embark on this enriching journey together!

Chapter 1: Decoding Autism

"Though devastating at first, Autism isn't the end of the world. It's the beginning of a whole new one." - Anonymous

Receiving an autism diagnosis for your child can come as a shock, particularly if you're unfamiliar with what autism entails. You might have many questions about what the diagnosis means for your child, how their conditions will affect their quality of life and more. This chapter aims to answer these initial questions, helping you understand the Autism Spectrum and will help you prepare for the journey ahead. At the same time, the chapter will also debunk some common myths and misconceptions about Autism, enabling you to understand what this condition is not.

What Is Autism? Understanding the Spectrum

In common parlance, Autism Spectrum Disorder (ASD) is a neurodevelopmental condition affecting a person's ability to understand and make sense of the world around them. It's a condition that makes people communicate and interact with others differently. As its name implies, ASD isn't a condition with clearly defined symptoms. People with Autism have varying levels of communication difficulties, sensory perception, repetitive or restricted behaviors, interests, and social interaction. People with autism can have severe behavioral challenges, but this isn't a rule. This is why it's called a spectrum — it's to indicate that the condition presents differently in everyone.

The Autism Spectrum

The autism spectrum isn't linear, meaning it doesn't have a clearly differentiated sign from one end to the other. It incorporates many different autistic traits, which are ways the person's brain processes information. This is due to the changes their brain goes through during the developmental phase before birth. To put someone anywhere on a linear spectrum would mean that they simply can or can't do something neurotypicals can, which isn't true. For instance, someone who is labeled "slightly autistic" may be assumed to be able to handle challenges they simply can't because, while they don't exhibit symptoms like intellectual disabilities or extreme social awkwardness, they still struggle with organization and other executive functioning skills. When those around them realize this, more misunderstandings arise, leading to a belief that the person is more autistic and is unable to function as an independent individual when, in fact, they can — they just have to go about it another way.

For the same reason, it's easier to imagine the ASD spectrum as a prism rather than a line with two opposing ends. On this prism, the lines between skills like language, motor, sensory filter and processing, and executive functioning are blurred as they all interact with each other. Some of these behaviors cause difficulties in everyday life, while others are useful (and even more so than in neurotypicals). Each autistic individual will have a set of traits in the different areas of the spectrum (prism).

The areas that are not affected will function just as they do in people who aren't on the spectrum, although they might be affected differently by diverse circumstances. For example, a person might not have problems maintaining reciprocal conversations but will be affected by sensory overload in loud and crowded spaces, where they'll struggle to have conversations. In contrast, another autistic person might be unaffected by noisy and crowded areas but find maintaining conversations extremely difficult.

Another example of this would be a lack of verbal skills. For instance, an autistic person might be unable to communicate verbally, but they'll understand what's being communicated and respond in other ways. It shows that not every person with ASD will act, think, and feel the same way, and everyone is capable of exhibiting varying strengths and weaknesses.

So, overall, when you're considering how to move on after receiving the diagnosis of ASD, it's your child's particular needs that are truly important. There is no diagnostic method for what challenges your child will have or what strengths they can develop. The support you give them should focus on their needs and capabilities rather than on their challenges. This way, they can learn how to develop strengths that'll help them counteract their weaknesses and thrive in life.

The Journey Ahead

As a general rule, children on the spectrum have a combination of two kinds of autistic symptoms — repetitive or restrictive behaviors and inadequate social and communication skills. However, as it is a spectrum of disorders, these traits are made up of a broad range of afflictions, which can affect their language skills, cognitive abilities, and behaviors. Below are some of the ways Autism manifests in children. Keep in mind that children's symptoms may vary. Moreover, just because they exhibit a few signs, it doesn't automatically mean they're autistic. The following challenges are only described to give you a general idea of what your child might face in the present and future.

Social Behavior and Understanding Challenges

Children with Autism often struggle with understanding and implementing socially acceptable behavior. For example, they might exhibit -

- Lack of interest in what others are saying or showing them or a lack of interest in sharing whatever they find interesting.

- Inappropriate body language, facial expressions, or gestures — or even more commonly, avoiding eye contact —all of which are part of the nonverbal cues that make up the social aspects of communication.

- Fear of approaching others either because they are uncomfortable speaking to anyone or because they're afraid of being misunderstood (either way, they can come off aloof).
- Difficulty making friends with peers in school, playground, etc.
- Inability to understand other people's reactions and feelings.
- Phobia of being touched (avoiding contact will also seem like an unusual and off-putting behavior).

Issues with Speech and Language

Children with autism often struggle with speech and language comprehension. For example, they might experience delays in expanding their vocabulary, talk in an odd tone, pitch, or rhythm all the time, or repeat words and phrases out of context. Some of the repeated phrases may be part of "non-functional knowledge." They learned this information because they found it interesting, but because they don't know how to put it in context, they can't use it in conversation or recall it to solve problems.

They might also have trouble beginning or maintaining a conversation because they only want to talk about their interests or are uncomfortable talking to others. Some children also have trouble communicating their needs and desires through speech and resort to nonverbal communication. Others may not understand simple statements or questions, whether due to intellectual disabilities or simply because they ignore what's being said because they have no interest in listening. The latter is particularly true for irony and sarcasm. Children with autism often don't understand the subtleties of this type of communication.

Restrictions in Play and General Behavior

Children with autism often exhibit rigid or restricted behaviors in their interests and activities. For example, they might:

- Feel the need to move constantly, even if it's only rocking in place while sitting on a chair.

- Become preoccupied with a narrow topic of interest, sometimes involving symbols or numbers.

- Develop an obsessive attachment to unusual objects like keys, rubber bands, or light switches.

- Have a tendency for atypical postures or movements, or can be overly clumsy and either fall or knock things down repeatedly.

- Have an overwhelming need for routines and order because they can't stand changes, which makes them upset.

- Develop a fascination by moving objects, like spinning toys or parts of toys like wheels on the car.

- Experience further restrictions due to sensory overload — they might be okay with playing or performing a task, but if their senses get overloaded, they may shy away from the experience/task in the future.

Another issue children with autism often face is that they are less spontaneous in play than their neurotypical peers. Unlike children who aren't on the spectrum, children with ASD generally aren't as curious about their surroundings, and they can appear positively disinterested in what's going on around them. This often hinders their creativity, imagination, and critical thinking skills. They are also less likely to engage in group activities (especially games that require waiting in turn or imitating others or something).

Sensory Problems

Many children with ASD can either overreact or underreact to sensory stimuli. The latter manifests as a lack of response when being addressed (they'll simply shut out the person speaking to them and act as if no one is around them). Sensory overload causes overreactions, and even the softest sounds can cause alarm. When something loud pops up, it can be extremely upsetting for them. Some children might try to lessen the influence of these sensory inputs by covering their ears or making loud, repetitive noises to drown out the sound that triggers their sensory overload.

Children with Autism also tend to be highly sensitive to texture, smell, bright lights, and touch. Their reaction to these stimuli varies from cringing to a full meltdown. Alternatively, some children may seek more sensory input by interacting excessively with objects by touching, smelling, or even hitting them. In some cases, this can be turned into a strength, a skill that helps them cancel out the adverse effects of other symptoms. For example, a child with autism might feel safe and comforted by being surrounded by familiar textures they can touch as many times as they want, even when experiencing a sudden or monumental change in the environment.

While the symptoms mentioned are often present in early childhood, in many cases, they won't become obvious until later, when the growing social demands exceed the children's limited capabilities. When this happens, the symptoms cause difficulties in social, academic, and other areas of life. Alternatively, the symptoms might be apparent early on but are overlooked and are later masked by learned strategies. In this case, the symptoms won't cause as drastic difficulties as in the previous one, but can still hinder the children from thriving and developing into independent adults with a fulfilling life.

Further Challenges, Hope and Triumphs

While not strictly tied to Autism, the following symptoms may also represent challenges for children on the spectrum.

Emotional Difficulties

Children with autism often cannot regulate their emotions or convey them appropriately. The slightest stimuli can set them off, sending them into an intense emotional meltdown without any apparent reason. This typically occurs when they're stressed, so managing their stress level helps to prevent problems. Likewise, some children with autism tend to become aggressive or disruptive when feeling anxious but are calm and easygoing when they're happy. Others can appear unfazed by real dangers like standing at greater heights or walking in front of moving vehicles yet be petrified of harmless objects or even food.

Inconsistent Cognitive Skills

Children exhibit diverse levels of intelligence. Yet, even exceptionally bright children with autism may encounter challenges in honing essential cognitive abilities such as memory retention and focus. However, through employing effective strategies, they can enhance these skills and progress toward achieving their objectives. On the other hand, some children with autism excel in tasks requiring visual skills and memory, yet find abstract thinking tasks challenging.

Savant Skills

Some individuals with ASD have so-called "savant" skills, which are heightened abilities limited to a specific area or field of interest. For example, some children on the spectrum do exceptionally well in math, and some can even do highly complicated mathematical calculations in their heads. Others can be talented in cognitive skills like memorizing text or pictures after seeing them only once or keeping entire calendars (all important dates included) in their head. Yet other children have exceptional musical talent and can recite pieces after hearing them only once. Whichever their talent is, they can use it to their advantage when working on personal, academic, and, later, professional growth.

Co-Occurring Conditions

Children with Autism can also be diagnosed with another co-occurring condition, including:

- ADHD
- Language delay
- Depression
- Anxiety Disorder
- Obsessive Compulsive Disorder

- Eating Disorders
- Psychotic Disorders
- Epilepsy or Seizure Disorder
- Sleep Issues

Debunking Myths

To fully comprehend what Autism is, it's also crucial to have a fundamental understanding of what Autism is not. As with many other neurodevelopmental conditions, ASD is often misunderstood, which leads to misconceptions. Below are some autism myths debunked.

One Can Only Be Diagnosed with Autism as a Child

Quite the contrary, a lot of people are first diagnosed with Autism as adults. This is likely because the research on ASD is ongoing, and understanding the condition has only just begun to improve. Moreover, there is no biological marker that can be used to test and confirm ASD, like for anemia, for example. Healthcare providers can only rely on the symptoms, which sometimes mimic other conditions, leading to misdiagnosis in childhood. Sometimes, people get diagnosed later in life because their symptoms are aggravated due to stress or drastic changes in their life circumstances.

Autism Only Affects Boys

While ASD can affect girls as much as it does boys, girls are still less likely to get diagnosed early on. Boys are always thought to be more active and rambunctious from an early age, so parents are more likely to notice the lack of these behaviors and activities. Disinterest in the surroundings, play, or other activities in girls is often attributed to shyness and generally calmer temperament. In truth, both genders are just as likely to be born with neurodevelopmental disorders, including Autism.

Autism Prevents People in Forming Relationships

Although people with Autism can struggle with social interaction, this doesn't mean they can't form or maintain relationships with others. They can build strong and fulfilling social and emotional connections with their peers, friends, and family and have children without their condition hindering them. While some people on the spectrum enjoy social isolation from time to time, most prefer to form and maintain relationships, even if it takes a little more work. Despite their deepest desire to establish these bonds, they still struggle because they lack understanding of social cues. Moreover, misconceptions (like mistaking an autistic person's blunt, non-nonsense answers for rudeness) by non-neurodivergent people may lead to further difficulties in establishing long-lasting relationships. However, by working on interacting with others in different environments (including non-inclusive ones), children with ASD can learn how to thrive in social settings despite the challenges and misunderstandings they might face in life.

Vaccines Cause Autism

This myth has long been debunked, as there is no scientific evidence that would lead to any connection between vaccines and ASD. With children who are diagnosed at an early age, the appearance of symptoms often coincides with the vaccination dates, which may lead to the faulty assumption that the vaccine caused the child's Autism. ASD has been linked to genetic factors, meaning it's not something a child squares after birth — they're already born with it. Environmental factors like stress may aggravate the conditions, but they won't cause it to appear.

Key Takeaways

- Autism is a unique neurodevelopmental disorder encompassing a spectrum of symptoms, behaviors, cognitive abilities, and language and social skills.

- Some of the symptoms prevalent in young children with Autism are failure to respond to their names, preference for solitary play, and aversion to affection.

- Older children with autism manifest symptoms like avoiding eye contact, difficulty interpreting others' body language, inability to carry on conversations with others, and repetitive behaviors and words.

- Many children with Autism exhibit sensory issues and have varying verbal abilities (which can also change over time).

- For children on the autism spectrum, the earlier they receive the help they need to cope with their challenges, the better outcome they are likely to have — however, since not all children exhibit typical symptoms, and some symptoms mimic other conditions, some children will receive diagnosis only later in life.

- Depending on what end of the spectrum they are, people with Autism can thrive in different settings just as much as their peers who aren't on the spectrum - they can form and maintain relationships, find employment suited to their abilities, and become valuable members of society.

With this information in mind, you can continue onto the next chapter, which talks about the power of early action in detail, emphasizing the importance of taking the right steps to give your child the best possible start in life despite their ongoing challenges.

Chapter 2: The Power of Early Action

"Autism offers a chance for us to glimpse an awe-filled vision of the world that might otherwise pass us by." – Dr. Colin Zimbleman

This chapter is specifically dedicated to guiding you through essential steps to set your child's trajectory toward success. Understanding the positive impact of early intervention is the starting point. As a parent, you'll be in charge of embracing and incorporating strategies into your daily life that can actively shape your child's development. These are the proactive steps you take to make a lasting and positive difference.

Equipping yourself to identify signs of autism spectrum disorder (ASD) early is mandatory if you are seeking a positive developmental change in your child, as is recognizing when to seek help. Learning about key indicators that signal the need for intervention, monitoring typical developmental variations, and potential concerns will set you on a path of positive outcomes for your child.

In this chapter, you'll read real-life success stories of children with autism. Each story emphasizes the uniqueness of every child's journey and offers both hope and practical insights into the potential awaiting your child. You'll also uncover research and case studies highlighting positive outcomes linked to timely intervention. Your early and prompt action can significantly improve your child's cognitive, social, and emotional well-being.

The Significance of Early Intervention

This section focuses on the transformative concept of embracing early intervention. Intervening early in your child's developmental journey should be your first step. Early intervention isn't only about addressing challenges; it's about seizing the right moment to influence your child's development during their formative years.

Proactively Embracing Strategies

A proactive approach is all about understanding and implementing therapies that actively contribute to your child's particular needs. It involves knowing your child's strengths, challenges, and preferences and developing strategies that work.

Unlocking Your Child's Potential

Although early interventions mitigate challenges and allow your child to cope with their weaknesses, the goal is to unlock their potential. By recognizing and addressing developmental concerns early on, you create the right environment and set them up with the tools they need to flourish.

Navigating the Developmental Landscape

While always having a positive frame of mind is not always easy, you need to be vigilant to pick up the subtle signs that indicate areas of concern and seek professional guidance when needed. Here's how you can navigate this journey with confidence and purpose.

Building a Supportive Network

Besides embracing early intervention and keeping positive, you also need to have a supportive network. Whether it's working with healthcare professionals, educators, or support groups, creating a cohesive support system will help you be more effective. These connections can offer not only practical guidance but also emotional support, providing a safety net during challenging times and celebrating victories alongside you. Moreover, a diverse network can offer different perspectives and insights, enriching your understanding and approach to managing whatever life throws your way.

Recognizing the Signs

Although most children with ASD are diagnosed in their pre-teens and later, parents can recognize signs associated with ASD early. For example, babies with communication problems won't respond well to sounds, gestures, and social stimulation when compared to other babies of the same age.

However, remember that this is not conclusive evidence of having ASD. It's simply an indication that you should go for further assessment by a certified healthcare professional.

The signs of ASD vary in different age groups. For example, a three-month-old baby will show sensitivity to loud sounds, won't follow objects with their eyes, and will have limited facial expressions, to name a few. Likewise, babies from the age of eight months to a year can show signs such as limited crawling or they won't communicate clearly. Other signs include limited eye contact and limited movement.

Here are the signs of the autism spectrum you must know:

Up to One Year:
- Limited or no eye coordination and movement.
- Showing interest in surrounding objects rather than people.
- Won't respond when spoken to directly.
- Repeated hand or body movements.
- No Babbling.
- Poor language developmental skills.

Up to Two Years:
- Limited interest in interacting with their peers.
- Will show specific and only a few areas of interest.
- Stay isolated from social interactions.
- Develop behavioral issues.
- Repeating phrases or words without realizing the meaning of their actions.
- Eating only selective foods.

Over Two Years:

- Unpleasant reactions to environmental triggers like sound, light, taste, textures, colors, and smell.
- Repeating the same body movements or exhibiting repetitive behavior.
- Delayed speech development.
- Extreme reaction to changes in their routine or surroundings.

Attuned Observation

Observing your child is the first step to recognizing any signs linked with autism. Watch your child's behavior closely, the way they communicate and interact in social gatherings. This involves not just watching but truly understanding any subtleties that may reveal underlying signs of ASD.

Identifying Developmental Milestones

Understanding typical developmental milestones is another tool that can aid in early recognition. From the common words your child uses to communicate and their behavior, you know about your child's development better than anyone else. The first time your baby waves at you, their first step, and their first smile are all developmental milestones. While all children reach these milestones at their own pace, the age is generally similar for all children.

Communication Red Flags

Communication is one of the core aspects of development. You'll be examining potential red flags in language development, speech patterns, and social communication. If you get an understanding of the intricacies and signs of what goes into communication and when the milestones should be reached, you'll be able to take steps to develop the necessary therapies.

The communication flags to look for include the following:

- Limited use of gestures like smiling, clapping, waving, nodding head, or pointing to an object.
- Delayed speech development.
- Use odd sounds or an unusual voice.
- Won't communicate clearly and use a limited vocabulary.

Social Interaction Patterns

From subtle challenges in eye contact to nuances in collective attention and peer interaction, these social interaction patterns are some potential signs. Here's a list of some other social interaction patterns that call for further evaluation;

- The child doesn't pay attention to people trying to interact or won't respond promptly.
- The child doesn't like to share warm expressions with family.
- The child will avoid social interactions or sharing their interests with others.

Recognizing these social nuances makes it easier for you to understand your child's social world more profoundly and better contribute to developing an effective strategy.

Sensory Sensitivities

Keep an eye out for whether your child exhibits diminished or heightened sensitivities to sensory stimuli. Around 96% of children reported with ASD show hypo-sensitivities, whereas 4% are hypersensitive to various stimuli. Sensory sensitivities are a common sign of ASD, as mentioned earlier.

Understanding the intricacies of sensory processing lays the foundation for creating environments that cater specifically to your child's sensory needs.

Behavioral Patterns

Behaviors often act as silent communicators. Certain repetitive behaviors or intense focus on specific interests mean you are probably going to need further evaluation. The patterns to look for include:

- The child develops certain repetitive patterns that become rituals (constantly repeating the same thing over and over).

- Shows interest in unusual objects like rocks, doorstops, vents, a piece of cloth, etc.

- Indulges in activities and actions that limit their social interaction.

Collaborating with Professionals

Recognizing these signs is not the endpoint. Effective collaboration with professionals is crucial. Discuss your concerns with healthcare professionals, the teachers at school, and the specialists your child visits. Building a collaborative approach develops a comprehensive understanding of your child's developmental landscape, facilitating a more accurate and timely assessment.

When to Seek Help

This critical section highlights when you must seek help for your child.

Monitoring Developmental Milestones

These are the same milestones you read earlier in the section. You have to monitor your child's trajectory of growth in areas such as communication, social interaction, and motor skills. Monitoring these milestones makes it easier for you to distinguish between normal variations and potential concerns, providing a foundation for informed decision-making.

Trust Your Parental Intuition

Your intuition as a parent is a valuable guide. Trust your instincts and feelings about your child's development. If you sense something is wrong or if your concerns persist, acknowledging and acting on your parental intuition becomes crucial to getting help in time. This intuition is fueled by the special bond a parent has with their child. If there's anything that's not right for your child, your intuition will tell you. All you have to do is trust it when it comes to your child and seek the necessary assistance.

Impact on Daily Functioning

Assess how potential developmental concerns affect your child's daily functioning in academic, social, or hygiene activities. Understanding the practical implications will guide you on how urgent it is to get professional help and support.

Likewise, as your child engages with educational environments, be attuned to their experiences. Understand how they adapt to structured settings, interact with peers, and respond to learning challenges.

Communication with Healthcare Professionals

Besides knowing the signs and recognizing your child's developmental, communication, and social challenges, you should also work on sharing this valuable information clearly with healthcare professionals. Learn how to articulate your observations and concerns. Open and collaborative dialogue with pediatricians, psychologists, and educators can make it easier to start planning a therapeutic strategy.

Support Networks

As mentioned earlier, building a support network for your child can provide several benefits. Having a solid connection between parents, healthcare professionals, support groups, and teachers will boost your child's morale and create an environment of solidarity.

By understanding the key indicators, trusting your parental intuition, and having effective communication, you can navigate the path to support with clarity and purpose.

Navigating the Diagnosis Process

Step 1: Acknowledging Concerns

Begin by acknowledging any concerns or suspicions you may have about your child's development. Behaviors, communication patterns, sensitivities, and academic and social interactions are the main areas of concern. Trust your parental instincts and recognize the importance of seeking professional evaluation if you have persistent concerns.

Step 2: Researching and Choosing Healthcare Professionals

Research and choose healthcare professionals, psychologists, and specialists experienced in developmental assessments. Look for professionals who specialize in autism spectrum disorder (ASD) or related developmental concerns. Consider recommendations, read reviews, and make sure they match up with your child's specific needs.

Step 3: Initial Consultation and Information Sharing

Schedule an initial consultation with the chosen professionals. Prior to your first meeting, compile relevant information about your child's developmental history, behavioral patterns, and any specific concerns you've observed. Openly share this information with the professionals to facilitate a comprehensive evaluation.

Step 4: Comprehensive Assessments

Navigate the process of comprehensive assessments conducted by the professionals. These assessments will evaluate your child's cognitive abilities, language skills, social interactions, and motor skills. Be prepared for various evaluation tools such as standardized tests, observations, and interviews. The goal is to obtain a holistic understanding of your child's strengths and challenges.

Step 5: Collaborating with Multidisciplinary Teams

Recognize the collaborative nature of the diagnostic process involving multidisciplinary teams. Engage with professionals such as pediatricians, speech therapists, occupational therapists, and psychologists. Understand how each professional contributes to a comprehensive assessment, ensuring a more nuanced and accurate diagnosis.

Step 6: Emotional Coping and Seeking Support

Acknowledge and navigate the emotional responses that accompany the diagnostic process. Understand that receiving a diagnosis, whether confirming or challenging initial suspicions, can evoke a range of emotions. Stay calm and seek support from friends, family, or mental health professionals to cope with these emotions effectively.

Step 7: Reviewing and Understanding the Diagnosis

Review and gain a comprehensive understanding of the diagnosis provided by the professionals. Engage in discussions with them to clarify any questions or uncertainties. This step lays the foundation for formulating a targeted action plan based on the identified strengths and challenges.

Step 8: Develop an Action Plan

Collaborate with professionals to develop a customized action plan for your child. Understand the recommended interventions, therapies, and educational strategies that will support your child's growth and development. This plan should be tailored to address the specific needs identified during the assessment.

Step 9: Advocating for Your Child

Become an effective advocate for your child within educational and healthcare systems. Familiarize yourself with processes such as Individualized Education Programs (IEPs) and access community resources. Advocate for the support services and accommodations that will best serve your child's unique requirements.

Step 10: Continuous Monitoring and Adjustments

Commit to continuous monitoring of your child's progress. Regularly communicate with professionals and be open to making adjustments to the action plan based on your child's evolving needs. This ongoing collaboration ensures that interventions remain relevant and effective over time.

This detailed step-by-step guide focuses on providing you with a structured and informed approach to navigating the diagnosis process. Each step is crucial in understanding your child's developmental profile comprehensively and implementing targeted strategies for their well-being and growth.

Stories for Inspiration

Each narrative showcases the resilience, progress, and unique achievements of these individuals, offering genuine inspiration and practical insights to parents and caregivers.

Oliver's Sonic Symphony

Diagnosed with ASD at a young age, Oliver's world was enriched by a profound connection to music. As his parents knew his love for enchanting tunes, they opted to enroll Oliver in music therapy sessions. Through music therapy and exposure to various instruments, Oliver discovered his innate talent for creating intricate sonic landscapes. Today, Oliver, a budding composer, demonstrates that the language of music can be a powerful channel for self-expression and connection.

Maya's Tech Innovations

Maya, diagnosed with ASD in her early teens, found her calling in the world of technology. Throughout her childhood, Maya was a calm soul and would spend most of her time messing around with the computer lab at school. Her teacher recognized her talent for troubleshooting and advised her parents to introduce simple coding games as mental brain exercises. Immersed in the love for coding and programming, she developed a keen interest, which, after a few years, has ultimately led her to create innovative software solutions that streamline communication for individuals with speech difficulties. Maya's story highlights the unique potential within the intersection of technology and neurodiversity.

Ethan's Wilderness Exploration

Ethan, an adventurous spirit diagnosed with ASD, always found solace and purpose in the natural world. As a child, he spent more time playing in the backyard and loved nature. Guided by outdoor therapy programs, Ethan developed leadership skills and a profound connection with nature. Today, he leads wilderness expeditions, showcasing that unconventional environments improve personal growth and resilience.

Zoe's Theatrical Brilliance

Zoe's journey with ASD unfolded on the stage. Diagnosed in her pre-teens, she found her voice and confidence through theater arts. Zoe's magnetic stage presence and ability to convey complex emotions through acting reveal the transformative impact of creative outlets in promoting emotional intelligence and self-expression.

Max's Culinary Creations

Max, diagnosed early in childhood, discovered his passion for the culinary arts. Through cooking classes and mentorship, Max developed a flair for creating exquisite dishes. Now a celebrated chef, Max not only delights taste buds but also demonstrates how vocational pursuits can turn into fulfilling careers for individuals with ASD.

Key Themes across Success Stories

Passion for Growth: Each story shared here underscores the role of passion for growth. Whether in music, technology, nature, theater, culinary arts, or even everyday life activities, these children found their unique paths to success by following their passions.

Innovative Approaches to Learning: The success stories showcase innovative approaches to learning and skill development. Tailoring interventions to individual interests makes the learning experience effective and more engaging.

Inclusivity: Reading through these stories, you might have recognized the significance of community support and inclusivity. Whether through therapeutic programs, mentorship, or creative spaces, a supportive community is necessary for success.

Diversity in Neurodiverse Achievements: From technological innovations to culinary excellence, these narratives challenge stereotypes and demonstrate the vast potential within individuals with ASD.

Continued Growth and Adaptation: These success stories are not finite; they illustrate a journey of continued growth and adaptation. Children with ASD can evolve, learn, and contribute to society throughout their lives.

In sharing these unique success stories, the intention is to highlight ways your child with

ASD can flourish, each on their distinct and extraordinary path to success.

Here are some more case studies for a clear perspective:

Case Study 1: Mia's Language Leap

Mia was diagnosed with ASD at a young age and was lagging in speech and communication-related developmental milestones. Early recognition of these red flags and timely language intervention transformed her developmental journey for good. Through speech therapy and communication-focused strategies, Mia made a significant leap in her language skills. Furthermore, timely intervention facilitated communication and unlocked her social interactions, paving the way for enriched relationships.

Case Study 2: Noah's Academic Flourish

Most children with evident signs of ASD need timely educational interventions. Diagnosed in early elementary school, Noah faced academic challenges. With personalized learning plans, specialized teaching methods, and a supportive environment, Noah caught up with his peers and surpassed expectations, showcasing the power of targeted educational support.

Case Study 3: Olivia's Social Navigation

Olivia's journey underlines the impact social skill interventions can have. Recognizing her social challenges early on, Olivia was enrolled by her parents in social skills training and peer interaction programs. The result was a remarkable improvement in her ability to navigate social situations, letting her create meaningful connections with peers and enhancing her mental well-being.

Case Study 4: Ethan's Behavioral Harmony

Like some children with ASD, Ethan had severe behavioral issues, which were resolved through applied behavior analysis (ABA) and consistent therapeutic strategies. Ethan learned to manage challenging behaviors and cultivate adaptive coping mechanisms. Timely behavioral interventions and undivided support from the family improved Ethan's daily functioning and contributed to a harmonious family dynamic.

Key Themes across Impactful Cases

Early Identification: The cases highlight that early identification of developmental concerns is a crucial catalyst for positive outcomes.

Holistic Approaches: Successful interventions often involve holistic approaches, addressing various aspects of development simultaneously. Combining therapies, educational strategies, and family support creates a comprehensive framework for success.

Tailored Individualized Plans: The impact is magnified when interventions are tailored to the unique needs of each individual. Personalized plans yield more significant and lasting results, whether in language development, academics, social skills, or behavior management. When put into practice correctly, you'll achieve profound results and contribute significantly to making your little star's life easier.

Collaboration across Support Networks: The cases emphasize the role of collaborative efforts across support networks. The involvement of parents, educators, therapists, and healthcare professionals in a cohesive team enhances the impact of interventions.

Building Foundations for Lifelong Success: Timely intervention lays the foundation for lifelong success. Addressing challenges early on can help your ASD child develop essential skills, become more independent, and follow the path that leads to a fulfilling and meaningful life.

Key Takeaways

- Noting down the developmental milestones and any discrepancies will let you make effective decisions guided by early action.

- Knowing the signs children with ASD exhibit at different ages makes it easier to tackle these challenges and plan the right approach.

- Continuous monitoring of your child's behavioral patterns, social communication skills, academic performance, and daily activities is necessary.

- Sharing any discrepancies, you notice with healthcare professionals is crucial as it will be the foundation for management.

- After receiving a diagnosis, develop an action plan in collaboration with healthcare professionals, therapists, and teachers to get the maximum results.

If your child shows delayed development and isn't reaching age-appropriate milestones or behavioral patterns or has an issue that is affecting their physical or mental well-being, you'll know quite early on that you're going to need to take action. In the upcoming chapter, you'll be reading about taking the right steps to map your child's world, learn about behavioral changes, and create an environment that celebrates your child's uniqueness.

Chapter 3: Inside Your Child's World

"Autism is a gift wrapped in a mystery." - Keri Bowers.

Don't you wish you could make your child's life easier? It isn't always easy to understand what children with autism or teenagers are thinking or feeling. They struggle with basic communication skills and expressing their emotions. Many don't even have the language to articulate their thoughts. This makes it hard for parents to know what makes their child happy, sad, or angry.

This chapter focuses on the different skills you can teach your child to make their life easier. You will learn the concept of empathy and how it influences your child to become a compassionate and understanding person. You will discover how to identify their stressors, joys, and interests. You will learn how to develop language skills in your child and behavior strategies for easier communication. You will also learn to love and accept your child and celebrate their unique qualities.

Building Understanding and Compassion

About 50% of children with autism struggle with empathy. As a result, they may seem uncaring or cold when their friends or siblings are crying or in pain. They can struggle with social situations or reading facial cues, resulting in misunderstandings and constant arguments. Your child may come across as selfish or heartless when they simply don't know how to act in these situations.

Autism affects children's ability to develop empathy because they struggle with regulating their own emotions and don't understand what other people are feeling. However, like any skill, empathy can be taught, and with the proper training, you can reinforce this behavior in your child.

What Is Empathy?

Empathy is the ability to put yourself in another person's shoes and feel their emotions or understand their thoughts. For instance, your child's friend is crying because their dog died. Even though your child doesn't have a pet, they can still understand and sympathize with what their friend is experiencing and feel sad because a loved one is hurting. They can listen to their friend for hours talking about their dog without judgment.

This skill is essential in navigating social situations. It teaches your child to be understanding and compassionate to other people's needs and, in turn, develop genuine and deep connections with others.

These strategies are effective in teaching children with autism empathy.

Social Stories

Teacher and author Carol Gray has worked with autistic students for years. She developed a tool called "Social Stories," which are short stories tailored for children with autism to explain social behavior. You will find many of these stories and comic strip conversations to teach your child empathy and improve their social skills.

Labeling Emotions

Since your child may struggle to read facial cues or body language, you can help them to develop these skills. Show your child photographs of people exhibiting a wide variety of emotions and ask them to label them. This will teach your child to recognize what others are feeling and react accordingly.

Body Maps

After your child learns to recognize emotions, teach them to identify the physical sensations associated with various feelings on a body map. For instance, anger is felt in the head, arms, and chest, and sadness is felt in the head, chest, and gut.

This skill helps your child understand what others physically feel when experiencing certain emotions.

Use Puppets

Use puppets to show your child how to respond to other children's emotional needs. Once they learn the proper response, you can role-play different situations where the puppet can be hurt or crying, and your child comforts them. You can also use action figures to show your child how their favorite superhero acts in similar situations.

Use Scripts

Use scripts or hypothetical situations with your child to teach them empathy. Say their best friend fails an exam and feels horrible. Teach your child the appropriate ways to comfort their friend, what they should say to make them feel better, and what tone of voice and body language to use.

For instance, they can sit beside them with a sympathetic look and tell them calmly that it is just one exam and they can do better next time.

Explain to your child that they shouldn't smile or laugh when someone is sad or in pain. Teach them proper body language, like patting them on the back or hugging them when a friend is upset or grieving. Write down a few statements they can use in various situations, like "Are you OK?" How can I help you?" or "I am sorry you feel this way."

Model Empathetic Behavior

Your child looks up to you, and they learn proper behavior by watching you. Make sure to always respond with empathy around them to model positive behavior. For instance, if you see another child fall in the playground, help them up and ask if they are OK. If your child loses their favorite toy, comfort them and help them look for it.

If you are sad, tell your child how you are feeling and guide them to put themselves in your shoes. For instance, you are upset because you lost your car keys. Tell your child what happened and how you are feeling. Ask them to think of a time when they lost a toy and were sad and frustrated and explain that this is exactly how you are feeling right now.

Positive Reinforcement

Use positive reinforcement to reward your child whenever they show empathetic behavior. For instance, their sibling falls, and your child runs to ask if their sibling is OK. You can express your pride in them by saying, "I love how you ran to your brother's aid. That is very sweet of you." You can also allow them extra screen time, give them a treat, or buy them a small gift.

Mapping Your Child's World

"What makes my child happy?" This is a question that all parents ask themselves every day. They want to know what brings their little one's joy and what stresses them out so they can protect them. With most children, you can simply ask them what their interests are or what activities make them happy, and they will tell you all about their favorite toys, games, or stories. However, children with autism may not have the proper language skills to express themselves.

Parents need to map their child's world to learn what makes them tick.

Interests

When a child with autism finds something that interests them, they can spend hours completely engaged and focused on it. Your child can be interested in a variety of things like playing an instrument, painting, video games, sports, and reciting movie lines.

Your child won't come to you and say, "I want to join the football team" or "I want to take piano lessons." You will need to discover their interests on your own. Watch your child during their free time and see what they enjoy doing. For instance, if they spend their time doodling or drawing, they are most likely interested in art. In this case, you could enroll them in an art class. Or if they enjoy watching movies and reenacting their favorite scenes, encourage them to participate in a school play or take drama classes. However, if your child doesn't have any interests, expose them to a variety of hobbies like swimming, football, ballet, music, art, drama, computers, adventure camps, etc until they find their passion.

Some parents assume that children with autism will not enjoy taking classes or following their teacher's instructions. However, if your child finds something they enjoy, you will be surprised by their commitment and progress.

Your child is never too young to have a passion. Whether they are two or ten, once they show an interest in something, help them nourish it. For instance, if your toddler enjoys listening to music, expose them to different genres and artists.

Whether your child is verbally communicative or not, they still have interests and passions and can use them to express themselves. For instance, a child who is non-verbal can express their thoughts and feelings through art.

Joys

Every parent wants to see their child happy and thriving. Children with autism are usually stressed because of their daily struggles with navigating social situations. So, what can you do to bring joy into their lives?

Limit Your Child's Anxiety

Provide routine and structure into your child's life and avoid pushing them too far out of their comfort zone. This will be discussed in detail in the next chapter.

Notice Their Sensory Differences

Children with autism are extra sensitive to certain sounds, scents, and tastes. Make your child happy and comfortable by creating a relaxing environment at home for them that is calm and caters to their needs.

Help Them Navigate Social Situations

Make your child's life easier by explaining to them the different social rules using logic. For instance, don't just tell them, "Don't scream at people." Explain how being loud can upset people and hurt their ears. Tell them that people will listen to them when they speak in a calm and soft voice.

Reward Positive Behavior

Praising and rewarding your child's positive behavior will make them happy and proud of themselves. Make sure to mention exactly what it was they did right. For instance, tell them, "You will get extra playtime because you helped me make dinner."

Make Time for Play

Don't just focus on therapeutic or educational activities. Make time for play and fun games your child enjoys, especially physical activities where they can run around.

Find What Brings Your Child Joy

Similar to discovering your child's interests, observe them and find what activities or situations make them happy. Are they happiest when playing, reading, or spending time with friends? Once you find what brings them joy, add time for it into their schedule.

Stress

Children with autism are usually more stressed than others. Certain situations can trigger them, like unpredictable events, new sensations, unfamiliar thoughts or emotions, inability to read others' facial cues, and any disruption to their routine. Eliminating all stressors from your child's environment isn't always realistic because they will constantly face stressful situations at school or with friends.

It is better to teach your child how to cope with these situations. Tell them to practice any of these techniques when they feel overwhelmed and need to calm down.

- Take five deep breaths.
- Retreat in a quiet room in the house.
- Close their eyes for a few seconds.
- Read a nice story.

- Jump on a trampoline.
- Run around the yard for a few minutes.
- Count from one to ten.

Behavior as Language

Autism impacts your child's behavior and communication skills. Your child can struggle with having a simple conversation with their friends, making it difficult to keep friendships. According to a 2006 study conducted at Western Michigan University, multiple behavioral intervention models can be used to teach language to children with autism and have shown tremendous results.

Applied Behavior Analysis (ABA)

ABA is one of the most popular therapies for children with autism. It is a method that focuses on understanding and enhancing behavior. It follows the principles of behaviorism, which highlight the significance of behaviors and the external factors that impact them. ABA therapy aims to boost behaviors and decrease ones by carefully examining and adjusting environmental factors.

In ABA therapy behavior, analysts employ methods to evaluate behavior and recognize the connections between behavior and its triggers or outcomes in the environment, then create personalized interventions to encourage changes. These interventions are often carried out in one on one sessions and can also be applied in real life settings like home, school or community environments.

It modifies their behavior so they can easily navigate social situations by rewarding positive behaviors and ignoring negative ones. It is recommended that children with autism receive 30 hours of ABA therapy per week.

A notable aspect of ABA therapy is its focus on collecting and analyzing data to monitor progress and adapt interventions as needed. Behavior analysts consistently gather and analyze objective data, on behavior enabling them to make decisions based on evidence and refine treatment plans over time.

Sensory Integration Therapy

Sensory integration therapy focuses on hypersensitivity, one of the most common and frustrating symptoms of autism. It aims to assist people in managing their reactions and enhancing their capacity to process sensory information. This therapy typically involves participating in a variety of tasks and drills under the supervision of a therapist. These tasks may include swinging, bouncing on therapy balls interacting with textured materials and engaging in activities that activate senses.

The objective of Sensory Integration Therapy is to support individuals in adjusting to their environment enhancing their focus, behavior and emotional control and boosting their involvement in daily tasks. The therapy is often customized to address the requirements of each person considering their preferences. Children sensitive to sensory stimuli like light or sound may be slowly exposed to more intense stimulation until they learn to cope with it.

Relationship Development Intervention (RDI)

RDI focuses on social behavior, such as making eye contact, reading facial cues and body language, and making conversation. A therapist first evaluates your child's needs and then sets appropriate goals. Parents then work with their children to achieve those goals while constantly communicating with the therapist and updating them on the child's progress. The therapist will then give the parents feedback on which areas require improvement.

Besides behavioral intervention models, other techniques can develop language skills in children with autism.

Developing Language Skills in Children with autism

Most children develop language skills from early childhood by watching their parents and playing with others. However, children with autism are more focused on the world around them instead of what people are saying. For instance, an autistic baby will be more interested in a ceiling fan than their parents laughing and playing with them.

So, parents will have to exert extra effort to develop language skills in their children.

Model Language Skills

Modeling language is speaking while using gestures and facial expressions. For instance, you can always comment on what you are feeling throughout the day. Say someone keeps honking at you while driving. You can frown and say, "I am angry." You can also comment on what you or your child are doing. You can say "Drive" as you drive the car, "Open" as you open the house's door, or "Drop" as your child drops a ball while playing.

If you feel your child is struggling to communicate something, model the words you think they want to say. For instance, if they can't open a bag's zipper, you can say "Help" so they know this is the appropriate word when they need assistance.

Only use short phrases that aren't longer than two words with children who aren't talking. However, if your child is speaking, model language by repeating what they say while adding two or three extra words to show them how to build long sentences.

Teach Language Skills during Play Time

Take advantage of playtime to teach your child language skills. For instance, you can do a jigsaw puzzle and only hand your child a piece when they ask for one. Make time for games every day where your child can have fun and learn at the same time.

Create Opportunities to Use Language

Create motivating, meaningful, and regular opportunities for your child to practice language skills. For instance, you can put their favorite toy on a top shelf, so they have to come to you and ask for help. Or you can make them popcorn without salt or caramel, so they ask for it. You can bring your child picture book flaps and encourage them to open them and talk about what they find. Make sure to give your child space and time to find the right words to articulate what they are thinking.

Once you notice progress in their language skills, make the activities harder. For instance, when your child wants water, start with them just saying "water," then encourage them to say "a glass of water."

You can also teach your child to greet you and their siblings with a wave or a high-five. Next, they can learn to say "Hi" and then "Hi, how are you?" and so on.

Positive Response

Respond positively whenever your child uses language skills. For instance, when they ask for water, give it to them right away. When they show you their toy, smile and make a nice comment. Don't look at your phone or let anything distract you. Show your child you are interested in what they are saying and give them your undivided attention.

Acceptance and Love

Your child isn't sick, strange, or different. They are unique and special in their amazing way. Children with autism have many positive traits like critical thinking, honesty, intelligence, and being non-judgmental, which make them wonderful human beings. However, many parents focus on the negative side of autism and ignore all its positive aspects.

Value all your child's autistic characteristics and always express how proud you are of them. Celebrate how your child is a lovely person who is incapable of manipulating others or telling a lie.

While others may struggle with understanding your child or seeing them as different, remind them they are unique. Their autism isn't holding them back, but it's making them better and stronger people.

Accept your child for who they are. Don't judge them or show frustration when they face challenging situations or struggle to understand emotions. Instead, support them and let them know that you will always be there for them.

Understand that autism is a part of who they are, but it doesn't define them or make them any less valuable or unworthy of love. When you love and accept your child for who they are, this will raise their self-esteem and teach them self-acceptance.

Key Takeaways

- Children with autism can learn empathy through various strategies.
- Empathy can help your child develop close and meaningful relationships.
- Parents are role models, and children can learn empathy from them.
- Using rewards encourages children to continue positive behavior.
- Observing your child can teach you about their interests and stressors.
- Making your child comfortable and limiting anxiety triggers can make them happier.
- Teaching your child coping skills is more effective than eliminating stressors.
- Behavioral intervention models can teach language skills to children with autism.

- Parents can help their children's language skills by using simple and effective techniques.
- Parents need to learn to love and accept their children with autism and be proud of their unique traits.

When you step into your child's world, you will discover a wonderful and lovely human being who is just lost and looking for help. You can support them by teaching them all the skills they need to easily navigate social situations.

Teaching your child empathy will make them compassionate individuals whom others feel comfortable around. Language skills will also make communicating their emotions and needs easier for your child.

A parent's job isn't just to teach their child certain skills. You should also create a comfortable and structured environment for them to encourage progress and growth. Head to the next chapter to discover how to create a peaceful and relaxing home for your child.

Chapter 4: Creating a Foundation

"Home is, I suppose, just a child's idea. A house at night, and a lamp in the house. A place to feel safe." - V. S. Naipaul.

What does a home mean to you? Does it represent safety, comfort, love, or all these meanings together? A person's home is always their haven, the one place they can feel safe, unwind, relax, and be themselves.

Children with autism are usually stressed at school as they struggle with sensory stimulation, changes in routine, and communication. Your child should return home to a comfortable and peaceful environment where they will feel in control of their surroundings.

Parents can't always protect their children from stressors in the outside world. What they can do is create a safe space for their child where they can grow, thrive, and feel safe.

This chapter explains how to create a structured environment for your child that allows for growth and comfort. You will also learn how to create a routine for them to establish consistency, and you will discover the power of positive reinforcement.

Structuring a Home for Comfort and Growth

Creating a comfortable and loving home for your child is vital to their wellbeing. Children with autism need a supportive and calm home environment in which to grow and improve. They don't fare well in unpredictable situations and require everything to be structured and organized to reduce stress and manage their behavior.

Reduce Sensory Stimuli

Seeing as your child is sensitive to sensory stimuli like light and noise, you should reduce or eliminate these elements to create a calm and stress-free environment.

- Install low-level lighting.
- Buy them noise-canceling headphones.
- Remove bright or harsh lights at home.
- Don't listen to loud music when they are around.

- Avoid loud activities.
- Buy them weighted blankets or chew toys (children use them to regulate their emotions).
- Provide relaxing activities like reading or coloring-in.
- Create a private and safe space they can retreat to when overwhelmed.

Provide Different Options

Children with autism need to feel in control over their environment. Offering your child different options to choose from in some areas of their lives and getting them involved in making decisions will increase their motivation at home and school. They won't only feel in control but will also have the chance to express their interests. They will feel supported at home, which will strengthen your bond with them. Children with autism who make their own choices are usually less anxious and stressed.

Create choice boards to encourage your child to make decisions. These boards are ideal for children struggling with verbal communication. Simply get a whiteboard and draw or stick different items on it for your child to make a choice. This technique is better than writing since visual aid makes the process easier for them.

Offer your child choices in these areas of their lives.

- Choose what to wear.
- Choose where to go on the weekends.
- Choose rewards.
- Choose snacks.
- Choose what to have for dinner.
- Choose between two games or activities.

When your child feels that they can choose for themselves and make their own decisions, they will feel empowered and confident. You are also preparing them for the future by teaching them to be independent and learn that there are consequences for every choice they make.

Make sure to provide your child with realistic choices, ones that you can deliver. For instance, don't ask them to choose between going to the zoo or the beach when you live far from the beach and don't have time to drive there. This can cause great disappointment and make them feel that their opinion doesn't matter. It could also affect their trust in you.

Encourage Structured Play

Toys and games aren't just for fun. They are also crucial for children's development. Playtime can improve creativity and imagination, boost physical fitness, encourage independence, improve literacy, build social skills, and develop cognitive growth. However, children with autism may struggle with certain types of games, especially if they have difficulty communicating. They may not be able to respond to others, follow instructions, share objects, take turns, or understand what other children are feeling or thinking. In this case, parents should consider structured play.

Structured play is when parents join their children during playtime to offer guidance and direction. You can encourage your child to learn play skills like sharing and interacting with their friends. Structured play is straightforward with its guidelines since it doesn't offer multiple scenarios that can overwhelm your child. It also makes ideas, steps, activities, or skills clear, helping the child achieve the activity's goal.

Structured play creates predictability, which reduces your child's stress and anxiety, making them more comfortable. So, they will be able to have fun with their friends and enjoy the game. Over time, your child won't require your assistance and will be able to finish the game by themselves.

Structure Play Technique

- Structure a game or activity by providing a beginning, middle, and end.

- Choose an appropriate activity for structured play, like matching games, bingo, coloring, or puzzles.

- Provide steps and instructions with visual support.

- Practice the steps one at a time.

Tips for Structured Play

- Choose activities and games appropriate for your child's development stage.

- Choose games your child will enjoy, encouraging them to play.

- Incorporate your child's skills and, more particularly, their strengths into the activity. For instance, if they are good at putting things together, play puzzles. If they can count, find ways to add math to the game.

- Don't force them to participate in the game, or they will feel overwhelmed. Encourage them, but let them come to you at their own pace.
- Only talk when necessary to avoid distracting them.
- Try to keep the activities short. Your child may lose interest if the game has multiple steps.
- Let them master one activity or game at a time.
- Cheer for them when they do something right, and celebrate when they win.

Home Sweet Home

Your home should be the safest place for your child. You shouldn't worry about them when they go to the bathroom by themselves or run around the house. Most parents reduce the risk of accidents by childproofing their homes. However, with children with autism, you need to take extra precautions. You will need to consider your child's unique behavior, cognitive impairment, and the severity of their condition.

You will have to go beyond regular childproofing. Remember, you aren't only protecting your child from harm but also adapting your home to their needs. You want to make them feel physically and emotionally secure.

Install Sophisticated Locks

Some children with autism can be very curious and want to know what's behind every door or inside every closet or drawer. If they find bug spray, paint, lawn fertilizers, or household cleaners, they may be tempted to taste them.

Protect your child by keeping all harmful substances in one place that isn't easily accessible to them, like the garage, and keep the door locked. However, this solution won't be convenient with items you use every day, like your child's medication. You may want to keep them in the medicine cabinet and childproof them, but some children are clever enough and can learn to unlock cupboards.

Your best option is to install sophisticated locks, especially if your child doesn't understand safe boundaries. They may be more expensive, but you can't put a price on your child's safety.

Be Careful of Regular Household Objects

Have you observed your child frequently bumping into objects or experiencing falls? Children with autism often grapple with sensory issues that contribute to clumsiness and an increased risk of accidents. Everyday items like hard floors, countertops, and furniture pose potential hazards.

To safeguard your child from injuries, consider securing tall furniture to the wall to prevent tipping and install rubber bumpers for added protection. Carpeting or non-slip mats can help prevent slipping accidents. In the kitchen, it's essential to use stove and drawer locks to prevent access to sharp objects and maintain clutter-free countertops to minimize sensory overload and distractions.

Create a Safe Space for Your Child

When a child with autism feels overwhelmed, they can resort to self-destructive behavior like biting themselves or banging their heads. To protect your child from themselves, create a safe space for them where they can relax and regroup. This can be their bedroom, a quiet corner of the house, or a small tent just for them. It should be a serene space with no distractions and away from other family members.

Either choose a space with no hard surface, like a tent or fort or cover the walls to prevent accidents. Decorate the space to your child's liking. Add blankets, their favorite toys, soft pillows, and anything else they need to calm down and regain their peace.

Whenever your child has a meltdown, redirect them to their safe space. In time, they will learn to go there by themselves whenever they need to take a break from the chaos around them.

Teach Them to Be Wary of Strangers

It isn't enough to secure your home; you should also be wary of dangers coming from outside. When your child gets older, they will usually respond when someone is at the door. For children with autism, this can be a very risky situation.

According to a 2013 study conducted at Sun Yat-sen University, children with autism are extremely trusting. Since they can't read facial expressions, they can't determine whether a person is trustworthy or not.

You should teach your child to never trust strangers, even if they come knocking at your door. Tell your child to never let a stranger in the house or go anywhere with them. They need to call you right away to come to the door and handle the situation yourself.

Knowing your child is safe at home will give you peace of mind so you can focus on supporting and nurturing them.

Consistency Is Key

Children with autism thrive in a consistent environment, and having a routine prevents emotional outbursts, reduces stress, and creates order in your child's life. According to a study conducted by pediatrician Dr. Elisa Muniz, children who grow up with a routine are more socially and emotionally advanced.

Significance of Routine in a Child with Autism's Life

- Lowers anxiety.
- Develops time management skills.
- Eases transitions between activities.
- Creates structure.
- Promotes predictability.

You can easily create a daily routine for your child using the C.A.L.M. strategy.

Create

Before creating a routine, write down all the tasks you want your child to finish. Make sure to assign specific hours for each task and determine how long each one will take based on your child's skills. Create the routine on a colorful sheet and add smiley faces or fun drawings next to each task. You can also add funny pictures of your child as well or pictures of their favorite cartoon character or superhero. Who said that a routine should be boring? Get creative and have fun with it.

Alert

Make sure your child sticks to the routine by setting an alert on your phone for each task. Let them know that these alerts are for them so they can recognize the sound and perform the task right away. Use a different tone for each task and make them fun, like animal sounds. Use a timer so your child knows the duration of a task. For instance, set two minutes for brushing teeth so they know when to stop. Over time, your child will recognize each task's tone and perform the task without you reminding them.

Like

If you want to encourage your child to stick to the routine, reward them with praise or small gifts. Make sure to tell them they are doing a good job and you are proud of them for finishing their chores. You can also add a thumbs up or a star next to each task they complete. At the end of each week, write on the schedule, "Good job."

Communicate with your child and discuss the routine together. Explain the significance of following a schedule and invite them to ask any questions. Teach them to go through each task in order.

Maintain

It can be challenging to maintain a daily routine, especially with young children. However, consistency is key. It will be easier for your child to maintain a schedule when they stick to it for long periods.

Once they adapt to their routine, they add new elements gradually. For instance, you can remove alerts to get them used to doing their tasks without reminders or encourage them to follow the routine when they visit their grandparents or other family members.

Track your child's progress by monitoring how long it takes them to finish each task, how many tasks they complete every day, how motivated they are when performing them, etc.

Celebrating the Wins

All children love praise. Their faces light up when their parents thank them for doing something or express their pride in them for a job well done. If you want to reward your child for completing their tasks or showing empathy when a friend is struggling, use positive reinforcement.

Positive reinforcement is a part of Applied Behavior Analysis (ABA) therapy, and many parents use it to reward positive behavior, improve their capabilities, or teach them new skills like:

- Verbal communication
- Non-verbal communication
- Social interactions
- Life skills
- Learning skills
- Academic performance

Make it a habit to constantly reward positive behavior, even if it's just with praise.

Positive Reinforcements vs. Bribery

Some parents dislike using positive reinforcement because they associate it with bribery. However, there is a difference between the two. Bribery comes before your child performs a task, and the child may not even complete it because they already have what they want. Positive reinforcement, on the other hand, comes after the task is completed. It is a reward that they earn for doing a good job. It gives the child a sense of accomplishment.

ABA Therapists and Positive Reinforcements

ABA therapists use a model called ABC to modify children with autism's behavior. They will monitor your child's behaviors and actions to identify the factors and triggers that impact them. They then organize their findings using the ABC model.

- **Antecedent:** The therapist recognizes the object, person, or situation that prompted your child's behavior, like loud noises or a bad scent.

- **Behavior:** Next, they will evaluate your child's reaction to the triggers. This reaction can be positive or negative.

- **Consequence:** This is the result of the child's behavior. It can be negative and prevent problematic actions or positive and promote good habits.

So, how can you apply positive reinforcement?

Identify Your Child's Needs

First, you should assess your child's social, academic, and behavioral skills. Write down all the areas that require improvement. Next, you should discuss your findings with an ABA therapist and work together to create a management program for your child.

Choose Reinforcements

Choose the most effective rewards and reinforcements that bring desired results. You can do this by trying different things to see which will work. For instance, praise your child after they finish a task or behave positively and see how they react. If they look disappointed or discouraged, give them a treat.

Examples of Positive Reinforcements

- Tokens like taking them on a fun trip if they stick to their schedule for a month.
- Privilege, like letting them choose what to have for dinner or where to go on the weekend.
- A toy they have wanted for a while.
- Food like treats or sweets.
- Verbal praise like "You are doing great."
- Extra play or screen time.
- Fun activities like going camping with the family or going to a sleepover at a friend's house.

Measure Progress

Assess your child's progress over time by asking these simple questions:

- Are your child's communication skills improving?
- Has their behavior improved?
- Is their social life thriving?
- Have their academic skills gotten better?

You can also track their improvement in other areas as well.

Rules for Applying Positive Reinforcements

- When starting, reward your child every time they complete a task or behave in a certain way.
- Once your child adapts to a certain behavior, gradually reduce the reinforcements.
- Use verbal praise with other types of reinforcements like toys or treats.
- Over time, you will only rely on verbal praise.

Key Takeaways

- Reducing stimuli and giving your child control over their choices lowers their stress and anxiety.
- Structured play creates predictability and prevents children with autism from feeling overwhelmed.
- Securing your home will protect your child emotionally and physically and give you peace of mind.

- Creating a routine and encouraging your child to stick to it creates a predictable, controlled, and structured environment that allows them to thrive.
- Celebrating your child's wins using positive reinforcement can have a huge impact on their behavior.

Creating a structured environment for your child is one of the most effective ways to help them manage their symptoms. When your child lives in a safe and organized environment and follows a routine, they will be happy and flourish. Show your child that you are aware of their progress by rewarding their positive behavior.

Some children with autism can't communicate verbally, so they rely on nonverbal communication. This can be challenging for parents who don't know how to reach out to their children. Head to the next chapter and discover how to communicate beyond your words.

Chapter 5: Beyond Words

"The most important thing in communication is hearing what isn't said." - Peter Drucker

Raising an autistic, nonverbal child will add further challenges to an already trying situation. You may feel like you can't communicate with your child, can't assess their needs, soothe them when they're upset, or teach them how to cope with their difficulties. However, there are many ways to communicate with nonverbal children, make them heard without speech, and build a loving, healthy bond with them.

This chapter outlines some of the best tried and tested methods of connecting through nonverbal communication, including strategies for establishing a form of language between parent and child, communication through play, and overcoming sensory issues while building a relationship with your child.

Connecting through Nonverbal Communication

Nonverbal children with autism have limited language skills, ranging from using some words to not speaking at all. Still, communication is critical for any parent, and this is no different for parents of nonverbal children with autism. Your child will want to convey their thoughts, feelings, and needs, so you'll need to learn how to connect to them through nonverbal communication techniques. These might include body language cues, sounds, movement, and other ways of self-expression. Some children with autism can learn to sign, type, or even write to convey what they want to communicate to the outside world.

Another challenge you might face is your child's difficulties with social interaction. For example, if your child struggles with engaging in conversations (even nonverbal ones), whether due to fear, awkwardness, or inability to read and interpret social cues, this will make communication even more troublesome.

Each child with autism is different and will respond differently to various communication efforts. Therefore, you need to find a form of communication that works for both you and your child. Moreover, establishing communication with a nonverbal child with autism is often a group effort, meaning it's a good idea to involve your child's therapists and teachers, too, so they can help you reinforce the strategies you are using to communicate with your child.

The Language of Love

As established previously, communication doesn't always involve speech, so understanding nonverbal cues is fundamental for your child's growth and development. The key is showing them you're there to help them express their needs. Your child needs to know that they have a way of telling you they understand you or ask any questions about what you're telling them. With techniques that convey your thoughts and feelings in a way you and your child both follow, you can establish a strong and loving bond. Below are some strategies to help you understand your child's needs with communication and establish the language of love that fits you both.

Always Pay Attention

Pay attention whenever you're around your nonverbal child. Even if it seems they're not communicating directly with you, their actions and reactions to their environment can hint at how they prefer to express themselves. For example, certain sounds to indicate specific situations, a cry, or a gesture made in a particular manner could express they want or need something.

Join in on Conveying Nonverbal Cues

Nonverbal social cues (like making eye contact or hand gestures) are widely recognized forms of interaction between people. For example, by pointing at something, you indicate that the person you are conversing with needs to pay attention to whatever you're pointing at, while smiling conveys happiness or contentment with the situation. If your child displays some of these nonverbal cues, join in with your own gestures. Make sure you exaggerate them to get the child's full attention and teach them body language skills that can pave the way for future communication.

Share Your Child's Interest

Beyond paying attention to their gestures, cues, and noises, also look closely at their interests. Does your child have a specific game they like to play frequently, a toy they can hardly let go of or play with uniquely? If yes, show interest in these activities by narrating what your child is doing. For example, if the toy is red, say, "You're playing with the red ..." or, "The red... does/go (whatever activity they're performing with the toy)." Your child doesn't need to use speech to build their vocabulary, and this strategy will help them learn more words they can convey through nonverbal communication.

Imitate Their Actions

When you imitate your child's actions, you acknowledge they're trying to communicate, and it reinforces respect in your relationship. You can copy the sounds they make and how they interact with their surroundings, showing you're keen to engage with them and that they can rely on you when trying to convey something they can't express verbally. For example, if you notice they like to arrange their toys in a certain order, do the same in front of them as soon as you notice the toys aren't in the "preferred" order. Or, if your child laughs every time they see an animal on the TV, make sure you laugh too. Besides encouraging them to share their emotions the best way they can, this strategy teaches your child about taking turns. It encourages them to pay more attention to what you're doing or saying to understand your nonverbal cues of facial expressions, sounds, gestures, etc.

Use Visual Cues

Using visual aids like flashcards can also make it easier for you to work out what your child is trying to convey to you. These visual aids can also teach new words (flashcards depicting everyday objects are particularly recommended). When showing a flashcard, point to the card and the actual item in the room. Repeat this several times, and if your child likes using the cards, get them to practice with them by pointing to a card whenever they need the object it depicts.

Gestures can also serve as valuable as visual language support for communicating with nonverbal children with autism. When giving instructions, back them up with simple gestures like showing the action you want them to repeat or pointing to the object you want them to get/use. Besides helping you convey crucial information to your child, this technique will also encourage them to use similar gestures to express their needs and wants. If, during your observation, you've noticed that your child has already started to use gestures of their own, make sure to incorporate these into the communication as well. When incorporating gestures, use them alongside keywords and not full sentences. For example, when teaching them to put on their jacket, point to it right when you say "jacket" in the sentence. Repeat the sentence and the gesture once, then only keep repeating the gesture and the keyword to make it easier for your child to understand. Repeating the sentence all over again could cause them to lose interest, while repeating only the keyword and the gesture will ensure they remain focused on what they need to do.

Schedules are often recommended as a visual aid for children with autism because they need structure. However, visual schedules can be even more helpful when you're trying to establish communication with a nonverbal child. Schedules typically contain predictable words and phrases that serve as reminders for a child. By having their schedule displayed in a visible place, they'll learn their routine without you repeating it to them repeatedly (which is especially great if they struggle with language and speech). For example, you can have a nighttime routine displayed in their room to take them through the steps like taking a bath, washing teeth, putting on pajamas, and everything else they might need to do before going to bed.

Just Keep Talking

It can be frustrating to keep talking to a child who doesn't respond verbally, but this doesn't mean you should stop. Even if you feel like they don't hear/understand you, just keep talking to them. Address them by their name, greet them, and keep instructing them to do their tasks, both verbally and nonverbally. And most importantly, don't talk about them in the third person when they are right in front of you or express your frustration about their inability to express themselves verbally. They need to feel included and supported, as this will motivate them to keep working on whatever communication skills they can use. Moreover, in some children with autism, language skills and speech can develop later in life, and the support they receive during their nonverbal communication phase plays a crucial role in developing more advanced communication skills like spoken language.

Use Child-Friendly Language

Whenever you're talking to your child, whether it's instructing them to do a task or narrating what they're doing to widen their vocabulary, use simple words, short sentences, and child-friendly language. Always start with short, one-step instructions, like "Give me the green ball." Repeat the instructions and see if they perform the task. If they do, you can move on to two-step instructions, like "Put the green ball in the box, and give me the box."

Pace Your Speech

It can be challenging to ascertain whether your child understands what you're trying to communicate to them. They might understand you perfectly but struggle to respond clearly, making you wonder whether the method is working. To eliminate doubts about their ability to comprehend what you're telling/showing them, pace your speech to emphasize keywords. In practice, this means speaking a little slower than usual while maintaining the natural rhythm of your speech. When you get to the words that convey the most important part of the message, change/raise your tone of voice slightly. After giving a short instruction, wait for your child to process the information and respond to your communication. If they don't respond after a few seconds, repeat the instruction. If this doesn't work either, try rephrasing the sentence or using different keywords and cadence to convey the information better. Once you find the sentences, keywords, and pace that works, use only these, especially when giving instructions for tasks, activities, and routines.

Stay in Their Line of Sight

While communicating with a nonverbal child with autism, make sure you're always in their line of sight. They may be uncomfortable looking directly into your eyes. Still, they will likely look at your facial expressions and mouth movements, which will help them learn about these social cues and their use during communication. They'll learn to follow your speech and body language, which will benefit them when adopting their ways of communicating with the outside world.

Use Sign Language

Using sign language to communicate with your child can teach them how to express their needs and gain independence by learning to speak to others who use the same method. Besides the traditional hand gesture sign languages, you can also use language programs incorporating signs, speech, and symbols to convey information.

Use an Assistive Technology Communication Device

Nowadays, there are plenty of tech communication devices and apps available to promote communication in nonverbal individuals. Tablets with apps promoting communication are the most popular with children. They can help build your child's vocabulary, make connections between photos and real objects (just like flashcards), and encourage them to start using spoken language. When a child touches a picture of an object, they can hear the object's name said aloud and might start imitating the sounds they hear. Even if your child can learn a few words using this method, it will make it much easier for them to work towards growth and independence.

Provide Them with Feedback

As you become more familiar with your child's nonverbal language, you can start offering them feedback on their communication. Convey to them how you understood what they communicated to you. This will help them understand your assumptions and give them a chance to rephrase what they expressed if they think your assumptions are inaccurate. For example, if you notice they're smiling during or after a new game they played with you, you can say, "I see you're smiling. I think you like this game."

Playful Connections

Play is one of the most efficient ways to teach children how to communicate. When children play, their cognitive skills are most active, and this is true even for children with language, sensory processing, or social difficulties. Below are some tips on how to use play to communicate with your child.

Encourage Playtime and Social Interactions

Find interactive games you can play together, as these provide enjoyable opportunities for both of you to communicate. Don't get discouraged if your child doesn't like or isn't interested in some of the games. It might take trying a wide variety to eventually find those your child enjoys. Once you do, it will be well worth it. You can also use playful activities that promote social interaction, like singing, and activities involving physical touch, like shaking hands, tapping the other person on the shoulders, etc. During these interactions, always stay at eye level so your child can follow your instructions, and you can keep up with their reactions.

Have Dance Sessions

If your child loves music, encourage them to listen to, dance, or even play an instrument if they're interested. These are excellent ways for your nonverbal child to express their thoughts and feelings, but also for you to experience the world from their perspective. Plus, they'll have tons of fun and release some of the negative feelings they have due to their challenges.

Encourage Art

Art (even fun children-oriented art like finger painting and playdough shaping) is another fantastic way to help your nonverbal child express themselves. Besides promoting creativity, creating art improves children's motor skills and can be used alongside other communication strategies like flashcards. For example, after showing your child a flashcard and reacting to the name of the object it shows, you can instruct them to finger paint the object on a piece of white paper or shape it from a playdough.

Arrange for Playdates

Children with autism often struggle to play with their peers, opting for parallel play instead. Rather than engaging with others, they play beside them, remaining in their own little world. However, this doesn't mean you should give up on playdates altogether. When arranging for group playtime, plan for games that encourage social interaction, and make sure you participate, too. You can play the same games you play with your child when it's just the two of you (as you'll know they like these) and incorporate the other children into the required tasks. After taking your turn, and when your child takes theirs, encourage them to wait for the other children to take theirs.

Sensory Sensitivities

Children with autism with sensory sensitivities will find it even more challenging to convey their needs and feelings. For example, they might be unable to use some communication tools as these could trigger a sensory overload. Or, they might struggle to follow your instructions because they'll get overwhelmed by the different parts of it. Fortunately, there are ways to adapt to your child's needs and use communication methods that cater to sensitive children.

Use Toys and Items with Tactile Features or Sounds

Soft, grip-able toys, toys that emit sounds, and books with tactile features are all great reinforcers for helping nonverbal children with autism express themselves. These tangible helpers are great not only for encouraging interaction but also for motivating them to communicate more. Moreover, if they struggle with sensory sensitivities, using textures and sounds that are familiar and a known quantity can be reassuring when working on overcoming their challenges.

Limit Questions

Rather than asking tons of questions, focus on providing instructions and getting information through simple words, pictures, or gestures. Even if your child understands the questions, asking too many at once will overload their sentences because they won't know which one to respond to or how to put them in context. Limit your questions to a few short ones, and always show context. Use visual support as well to help the child understand. If your child doesn't understand your questions or doesn't know how to respond, rephrase the questions into short and precise instructions. For example, they'll be more likely to follow through with a message like, "Show me," than with a question like "What do you need/want?"

Offer Them Choices

If you struggle with understanding your child's needs, offer them choices. This will help you narrow down what they're trying to communicate to you. Offering choices will come in handy when dealing with a child with sensory sensitivities because by giving them a choice between something that might trigger a sensory overload and something safe, they'll know you understand their needs.

Provide visual aids to show your child what choices they have. It's also helpful to come up with an aid your child can use to signal if neither of the offered choices is what they want or need. For example, when asking what they want for a snack, you can show them flashcards or pictures in an app for apples, sandwiches, etc. Then, show them a sign that indicates "something else" — this should be a sign your child has learned previously so they'll know what it means. If they indicate they want something else, offer them further choices.

Listen More Than You Talk

Not only is it more helpful to wait for the child to respond to your communication, but quietly waiting will also help them focus on the question without pressuring too much and overloading their senses. When you ask a question or give instructions, allow your child plenty of time to think and respond in a way they prefer to communicate. In other words, you should listen more and wait quietly than talk to the child. While listening and waiting, you'll also have a chance to observe them to see how they process the information and begin their communication so you can follow their lead as you continue your conversation. When in doubt, count to 10 in your head to keep yourself from interfering and allow them enough time to respond.

Key Takeaways

- As challenging as it is to establish communication with a nonverbal child with autism, there are plenty of ways to overcome this obstacle and form a bond that goes beyond spoken language.

- Paying attention, imitating your child's cues, and backing them up with visual aids are great ways to encourage them to convey their wants and needs.

- Pacing your speech and staying in their line of sight will help your child remain focused on making connections between words and gestures.

- Encouraging playtime (especially with games involving social engagement) is also a great idea when establishing communication with nonverbal children with autism.

- Art and dance promote creative self-expression and can be combined with other communication methods.

- If your child struggles with sensory sensitivities, they'll benefit from communicating through toys and items with special features like tactile and soft surfaces.

Now that you've established communication with your child, you'll have a better idea of their needs and capabilities. The following chapter talks about tailoring the management approach specifically to your child's condition, which is the next step in building a powerful support system for them.

Chapter 6: Tailored Strategies

"It seems that for success in science or art, a dash of autism is essential." - Hans Asperger

As a parent, you only want the best for your child. Every child diagnosed with ASD shows varying signs and symptoms mainly linked to development and behavior. Crafting a personalized autism management plan is essential to address the issues your child faces. It's a process that begins with a thorough assessment of your child's needs and strengths. Although your child's healthcare provider will run several tests and evaluations, you will be the one monitoring their communication skills, sensory sensitivities, social interactions, behavioral patterns, and any other signs. Once the assessment is complete, the next step is to establish a management plan.

This involves getting together with your child's therapists and setting clear goals and objectives tailored to your child's individual profile while taking into account factors like preferred learning styles, sensory preferences, and existing skills. In this chapter, you'll read everything about crafting customized strategies, learn about the process, and find ways you can tweak them for the best outcomes.

Creating a Customized Autism Management Plan

Assessing Needs and Strengths

As several management strategies are available, it can sometimes take time to figure out the right approach. When putting a management plan in place, remember that there's no single strategy that works for everyone. Each child is unique and has varying needs and strengths. You already know areas your child may struggle in and where they excel. All you have to do is to keep these strengths and needs in mind when tailoring strategies. Moving forward, you need to establish clear goals and objectives. Here are the points you must consider when tailoring a customized plan:

- As mentioned earlier, know your child's strengths and weaknesses.
- Map out the behaviors that are causing problems.
- Make a list of basic skills and note down areas your child may struggle with.

- The way your child prefers to learn. e.g., Through listening, seeing, or performing it.
- Think about the activities your child loves and how you could use them in management to improve learning.
- Evaluate their communication skills, sensory sensitivities, and social interaction capabilities.

Consistency across Environments

Children diagnosed with ASD find it challenging to use newly learned skills or apply what they have learned across various settings like home, school, and other environments. For example, if your child uses sign language to communicate at school, encourage them to use it at home and make sure to keep their experience consistent for effective reinforced learning. You can even attend therapy sessions with your child and copy their techniques at home for better practice.

Scheduled Routine

Creating a scheduled routine for your child is like laying down a comforting and predictable path in the midst of life's sometimes chaotic journey. It will be your child's roadmap that guides them through each day and promotes a sense of security and stability. A scheduled routine is more than just a list of tasks; it's a carefully crafted framework that nurtures your child's development, encourages healthy habits, and creates a sense of control over their environment. Just like a well-rehearsed play, it can ease transitions, minimize stress, and enhance the overall well-being of your child. Picture mornings where getting ready for school becomes a streamlined process or evenings where winding down leads seamlessly to restful sleep. Establishing a scheduled routine is like setting the stage for a smoother daily life and enabling your child to thrive amidst the rhythms of their day.

Be Flexible

Keep your management plan flexible. Assess progress regularly, reevaluate your goals, and adjust strategies to accommodate the evolving needs of your child. For example, if they are not responding well to speech therapy, try introducing speech therapy exercises at home.

The information you'll gather through this comprehensive assessment will be the foundation of your child's customized management plan. Furthermore, it will become easier to implement intervention strategies that get to the heart of your child's challenges and allow their existing abilities to shine.

Aligning Strategies with Best Practices

Make sure your strategies are based on recognized best practices for autism because any other type of plan could have negative effects on your child's physical and mental well-being.

When integrating evidence-based practices, don't forget to consider your child's needs, strengths, and weaknesses. What works well for others may not work well with your child or may need adjustments before implementation. Lastly, don't hesitate to engage your child in another type of therapy if the current one is not producing results. For example, if occupational therapy is not showing positive results, try Applied Behavioral Analysis (ABA therapy) or Relationship Development Intervention (RDI).

Collaborating with Care Teams

No matter what type of strategy and management plan you choose, having everyone involved on board is vital. Creating a support team will require you to get educators, therapists, healthcare professionals, and family members all on one page. Encourage effective communication and information sharing among members to develop a comprehensive understanding of your child's needs and a unified approach to intervention.

You can use online communication platforms for regular team meet-ups and share progress updates, ensuring that everyone involved is on the same page.

Role Clarification for Specialized Input

Although you need to know about how different therapies work and the way they boost learning outcomes, there are some areas of the management plan that require expertise. For example, professional speech therapy sessions can produce phenomenal results.

Family Involvement for Continuity

Your active involvement in your child's life is a driving force that ensures continuity and success. Getting your family on board the management process makes it even stronger and connects home and school seamlessly to create a trigger-free life. The entire family's engagement in your child's learning journey will act as a catalyst for stability and understanding. The key here is to maintain ongoing communication with educators, sharing insights, strategies, and achievements.

Share Educational Materials

Imagine having access to information that sheds light on your child's condition and equips you with the tools to support their journey effectively. Start by providing your family with comprehensive resources that demystify autism, offering insights into its nuances and strategies that promote development. You can gather these educational resources from this book, your child's healthcare provider, from therapists, seminars, and from various credible online resources. Several organizations and leading healthcare professionals also host webinars from where you can get the latest developments on autism to share with your family.

In this tech-oriented age, you'll find valuable resources in a matter of minutes. Furthermore, it's easy to search and learn about any issue you are dealing with. For example, if you are finding it difficult to create a sensory-friendly home environment, search for a workshop or an online webinar on sensory processing issues in autism, and you'll find practical tips for better results.

Regular Family Feedback for Plan Adjustment

Regular family feedback to the collaborative team, especially your child's doctor, is the cornerstone for fine-tuning and adjusting strategies. With regular check-ins, you'll be sharing observations about your child's progress, challenges, and triumphs, forming the basis for adjustments to their developmental plan.

Tailored Strategies to Consider

Cartooning Strategies

Cartooning strategies involve leveraging visual tools, like social stories or comic strip conversations, for a visual narrative that aids in the understanding and navigation of social situations for children with autism. The strategy uses simplified drawings or cartoons to represent social scenarios, expected behaviors, and potential outcomes. Here's a scenario for clarity. Say your child got into a scuffle at school during break time and was sent to the principal's office. With the right support and tools, your child could draw the event as a cartoon, use speech bubbles to express themselves and learn from the experience.

To introduce this strategy, try creating a cartoon or a social story that involves breaking down complex social situations into visual components. The story may include characters, settings, and specific behaviors, offering a step-by-step guide to social expectations. The use of visuals taps into the strengths of visual learning, allowing children to grasp and internalize social information more effectively.

Modeling

It's a behavioral strategy that involves demonstrating desired behaviors or skills for the child to observe and imitate. This technique is particularly effective for teaching complex tasks or behaviors by providing a clear example for the child to follow. This demonstration breaks down the behavior into observable and replicable steps, making it more accessible for the child. Repetition and reinforcement are crucial to solidify the learning process, helping them generalize the modeled behavior to different contexts.

Peer Training

Peer training involves educating peers about the condition and explaining the kinds of strengths and challenges their classmates would have. The goal is to encourage positive social interactions, understanding, and inclusiveness. These sessions elicit empathy, reduce stigma, and equip peers with the tools to be supportive of their autistic classmates. Structured activities, discussions, and role-playing scenarios can be included to enhance understanding and create a more inclusive social environment.

Self-Management Techniques

Self-management techniques can help your child to independently regulate their behavior, emotions, and attention. Children are taught to recognize and monitor their own behaviors by using visual cues, checklists, or self-monitoring charts. The process involves setting clear goals, identifying target behaviors, and implementing strategies for self-correction. Reinforcement mechanisms, such as rewards or praise, are often integrated for motivation and encouragement. The goal is to make them independent in managing their own actions and emotions across various settings.

Social Skill Training

Social skill training is a systematic approach to teaching and practicing social behaviors with the aim of enhancing a child's social competence. The training breaks down social skills into specific components and provides structured instruction and practice. Each skill is explicitly taught through vocal instruction, modeling, and role-playing. Interactive scenarios and real-life examples are used in social skill training to reinforce understanding and application. Consistent practice in controlled settings helps generalize these skills to different social contexts.

Adapting the Plan

Recognizing the Need for Adaptation

Adapting an autism management plan exactly to your child's requirements is an essential part of providing effective support. Knowing when, why, and how to adjust the plan ensures that the plans you make remain relevant to your child's evolving needs. Let's say your child encounters a new social or is being frustrated by a sensory stimulant at home. You'll be the first to pick up on subtle cues like these. This recognition will be your roadmap, signaling when it's time to adjust and adapt.

When to Adapt

Keep a watchful eye for signals like a sudden affinity for a particular activity, a struggle with a specific task, or a shift in mood. These are prompts for you to act immediately and turn these situations into chances for growth.

Why Adapt

Adaptation is not about giving in; it's about making an experience that suits your child and helps them cope with challenges. It's like tailoring an experience to fit just right. Adapting is your way of saying, "I see you; I understand you, and I'm here to create an environment that supports you."

How to Adapt

Utilize the same collaborative support network and share information, engage in discussions, and brainstorm ideas. It's a collective effort to find the best strategies, whether it involves adjusting learning materials, modifying routines, or introducing innovative approaches that work perfectly with your child's learning style.

Here are some tips to make this transition streamlined:

- Observe keenly and keep a close eye on progress by comparing progress reports.
- If things are not going well, it might be time for more advanced help and a re-evaluation by the relevant healthcare professional.

- If there are challenges, tweak things to fit better.

- Always consider feedback from the collaborative team and family.

- Stay flexible with the strategies you implement.

- What helps one person with autism might be different for another. Change your approach based on what works best for your child.

- When reworking a plan, include things that make learning and therapy interesting and fun for you.

- Introduce changes to the management plan gradually. Abrupt modifications may cause stress or resistance.

Data-Driven Progress Assessment

Although you can keep a log of your child's progress concise, it's best to add every nitty-gritty detail. Imagine a roadmap for your child's progress that not only checks the boxes when they hit milestones but also a dynamic data-driven narrative tailored to their distinct requirements. Data-driven progress assessment for children with autism is a powerful tool, and you, as the parent, are at the heart of this journey. Following this approach, your child's development will be tracked through observations and tangible data points. Regular assessments, backed by data, highlight your child's strengths, areas of growth, and the effectiveness of your strategies.

Furthermore, with this approach, it becomes easier to fine-tune the plan. For example, if a specific intervention strategy is working, the data reflects this success, guiding educators and specialists in refining and tailoring future plans.

Celebrating Progress

Celebrating your progress and achievements, both big and small, can become the stepping stones to success. Don't hold back when you achieve a developmental milestone or when you are seeing clear improvement in areas where your child has had difficulty. These moments of triumph are benchmarks and reasons to celebrate the resilience and perseverance of your child. The process is not about highlighting deficits but recognizing progress and potential.

Key Takeaways

- Crafting a personalized autism management plan is crucial for addressing your child's challenges and for promoting development.

- The assessment phase involves your active participation in monitoring your child's communication skills, sensory sensitivities, social interactions, and behaviors.

- Collaborate with therapists to set clear goals and objectives.

- Flexibility and consistency are key elements.

- Align strategies with evidence-based practices for autism intervention, considering your child's strengths, weaknesses, and needs.

- Collaborate with educators, therapists, and healthcare professionals to create a unified support team for your child.

- Embrace Collaborative Problem-Solving as a transformative approach to address challenges, fostering a positive and supportive learning environment.

- Ensure family involvement for continuity, maintain ongoing communication with educators, and share insights, strategies, and achievements.

- Provide educational materials to family members, accessing resources that demystify autism and support your child's needs.

- Provide regular family feedback so the strategies in your child's management plan can be fine-tuned.

- Recognize the need for adaptation in the management plan, observe signals, adapt when necessary, and celebrate progress along the way.

- Utilize data-driven progress assessment to visualize your child's development and guide adjustments in the management plan.

- Celebrate progress, acknowledge achievements and resilience, and actively participate in the story of your child's developmental journey.

Chapter 7: Choosing the Path

In the course of choosing the right therapy, you'll find a wide array of options. From research-backed therapies like Applied Behavior Analysis (ABA) and Cognitive Behavioral Therapy (CBT) to more interest-based therapies like Equestrian therapy, music therapy, and play therapy, there's a spectrum of options to choose from. In this chapter, you'll be reading about the different therapies you can introduce, the considerations you need to keep in mind while making a choice, the areas to prioritize, and ways to integrate these therapies for a holistic approach toward management.

A Spectrum of Therapies

Applied Behavior Analysis (ABA)

As a parent moving through numerous autism management strategies available for your child, it's crucial to break down the options into manageable components. Here are some therapies to consider.

Applied Behavior Analysis (ABA)

Think of ABA as a structured playbook for your child's development. Applied Behavior Analysis is a method that dissects behaviors into small, achievable steps. The process is similar to the straightforward guidelines in structured play; ABA focuses on positive reinforcement and feedback to enhance communication skills, social interactions, and adaptive behaviors. Your child will work with a trained therapist to break down complex behaviors into manageable parts, making learning more accessible and practical. Through consistent positive reinforcement, your child can make significant strides in their overall development. Collecting the data of your progress and sharing it with your child's therapist is pivotal as insights from this data will help them to make adjustments to the intervention plan. This therapy is particularly effective in addressing various behavioral challenges associated with Autism Spectrum Disorder (ASD).

Speech Therapy

Speech therapists work closely with your child to improve verbal communication or explore alternative methods like sign language or visual aids. In this therapy, your child will engage in activities that target specific speech and language goals. The therapist will tailor exercises to your child's needs, making the learning process engaging and enjoyable. Your child exercises to strengthen oral muscles, plays language games, and practices social communication to improve communication proficiency.

Occupational Therapy

Occupational therapy addresses sensory challenges and enhances daily living skills. Therapists work collaboratively with your child to develop fine and gross motor skills, promoting independence in various activities. The therapy sessions include engaging activities designed to improve your child's ability to perform daily tasks, from buttoning a shirt to holding a pencil. By breaking down these tasks into manageable steps, occupational therapy contributes to your child's overall self-sufficiency and boosts their self-confidence.

Social Skills Groups

Just as in structured play, where interaction is encouraged, social skills groups provide a supportive environment for your child to practice and refine their social skills. These groups are structured controlled spaces where your child can navigate social scenarios with guidance and understanding. Trained professionals guide the group activities, ensuring that your child feels supported and encouraged to interact with their peers. This collaborative setting builds essential social skills in a structured and positive manner.

Much like your involvement in structured play, your active role is indispensable in your child's journey through autism management. Please remember that your child is an individual, and these therapies can be tailored to their particular stage of autism. Your consistent engagement and encouragement can boost your child's progress immeasurably.

Cognitive Behavioral Therapy (CBT)

Cognitive Behavioral Therapy (CBT), when implemented the right way, has the power to reshape thought patterns and behaviors that are interfering with your child's development. This therapeutic approach focuses on understanding and changing negative or unhelpful thoughts and actions.

CBT is goal-oriented and always aims for a specific outcome. A trained therapist works with your child to identify and challenge negative thought patterns, replacing them with more positive and constructive ones. Through a series of sessions, your child learns to recognize and modify these emotional challenges or disruptive behaviors.

Augmentative and Alternative Communication (AAC)

Just as speech therapy supports verbal communication, Augmentative and Alternative Communication (AAC) is a brilliant therapy for children with autism with limited or no verbal abilities to express themselves. AAC is like introducing a personalized toolkit for communication, offering various methods beyond spoken words.

The therapy includes tools like communication boards, gestures, sign language, and high-tech devices. The structured nature of AAC allows for gradual learning and implementation. Professionals work with your child to identify the most suitable AAC methods, considering their communication styles. Effective AAC therapy facilitates communication and encourages independence, self-expression, and social interaction for better engagement.

Just like you tweak structured play to adjust to your child's capabilities, CBT and AAC can be adjusted to meet ever-evolving, inquiring minds. Collaborate with therapists and specialists to create a personalized plan that can show you the way to integrate these approaches seamlessly into your child's daily life.

Sensory Integration Therapy

Sensory Integration Therapy is a specialized intervention targeting sensory processing challenges commonly experienced by children and adults with ASD. The therapy involves exposing your child to controlled stimuli in a structured and repetitive manner to let them adapt gradually and respond appropriately to the controlled sensory input. This therapy improves sensory integration, allowing your child to better regulate responses and engage more effectively in daily activities.

Early Start Denver Model (ESDM)

The Early Start Denver Model (ESDM) is an evidence-based early intervention approach designed to support toddlers and preschool-aged children with autism spectrum disorder (ASD). Much like the structured play framework, ESDM emphasizes play-based activities to encourage development across various domains.

ESDM follows a curriculum integrating behavioral and developmental principles. Trained therapists work closely with children, incorporating play activities that target specific goals, like communication, social interaction, and cognitive skills. It's an early and intensive intervention designed to enhance developmental outcomes and set a positive trajectory for a child's overall growth.

Music Therapy

This harmonious therapy utilizes the universal language of music to address developmental goals. A trained music therapist engages children in musical activities to encourage interaction, improve communication, and enable children to express themselves emotionally.

This creative music therapy involves activities like singing, playing instruments, and rhythmic exercises tuned to each child. The rhythm and melody create calming tunes to promote engagement and support the development of various skills.

Equine-Assisted Therapy

Equestrian therapy, or equine-assisted therapy, follows a distinct protocol for therapeutic engagement. While most therapies are conducted indoors or in controlled environments, Equestrian therapy takes place around interactions with horses. Through activities like riding, grooming, and caring for horses, children can experience physical, emotional, and social benefits.

The structured sessions, guided by trained professionals, create a supportive environment for achieving therapeutic goals. Your child's motor skills, sensory integration, and emotional regulation can improve significantly. However, remember that it's an outdoor activity, and children with sensory sensitivities may find this therapy setting problematic to follow.

Pivotal Response Training (PRT)

It's a behavioral intervention model targeting core developmental skills. PRT identifies key behaviors or "pivotal" areas, like motivation, self-initiation, and responsiveness to cues. During PRT sessions, therapists use naturalistic teaching strategies, incorporating the child's interests and preferences. Much like structured play, this approach aims to generalize skills across various settings, promoting flexibility and adaptability.

Lovaas Model

The Lovaas Model, rooted in Applied Behavior Analysis (ABA), is another intensive early intervention approach for children with autism.

Here, the ABA principles are applied systematically to address specific behaviors and teach new skills. The goal is to reduce challenging behaviors and promote the acquisition of functional skills through systematic teaching and reinforcement.

Physical Therapy (PT)

Focuses on improving motor skills, coordination, and physical well-being. PT sessions include tailored exercises to strengthen specific motor challenges.

Medications

In some instances, medications may be prescribed to manage particular symptoms associated with autism spectrum disorder (ASD). Medication interventions are not a standalone solution but may be integrated into a comprehensive management plan, much like how different elements are integrated into structured play.

Commonly, medications for hyperactivity, anxiety, or aggression are prescribed after extensive evaluation. Medication interventions are personalized, recognizing that each child's response may vary.

Most of the interventions listed above can be tailored to your child's physiology. If you are feeling overwhelmed, collaborate with the therapist and relevant healthcare professionals to create a comprehensive and individualized management plan based on your child's strengths, challenges, and preferences.

Understanding Your Choices

Conducting an individualized assessment of cognitive abilities, communication skills, sensory processing, and any coexisting conditions is necessary before choosing a plan. Professionals utilize standardized assessments, observations, and, in some cases, series of interviews to gather comprehensive information and act effectively.

After gathering these insights, prioritize specific areas that have a significant impact on your child's daily life. For example, your child might be facing communication challenges, social difficulties, sensory processing issues, or is unable to develop self-care abilities. Prioritizing these key areas makes it easier for therapists and caregivers to tailor interventions and address the most pressing needs, promoting targeted and practical support.

It's a no-brainer to engage family members in the assessment process so you can map their daily routines, preferences, and challenges better within the home environment.

Lastly, the therapies listed here and others are primarily age-specific. Always take into account the developmental stage. The management strategy you pick must be coherent with age-appropriate milestones and expectations.

Where to Start with Management Strategies

Once your needs are prioritized, create a strategic and phased approach. You should initiate interventions in a manner that builds a strong foundation for subsequent therapies and maximizes the strategy's effectiveness.

Targeted Therapies

Begin with targeted therapies. For example, if communication is a priority, speech-language therapy can be your starting point. Likewise, if behavioral challenges are prominent, Applied Behavior Analysis (ABA) could be initiated to address those specific concerns.

Integrating Therapies

With the right approach, combining therapies for Autism Spectrum Disorder (ASD) creates a holistic framework to blend in various management options to create a comprehensive and interconnected approach that addresses the diverse needs of your child with ASD. You can integrate behavioral, communication, and sensory therapies seamlessly, addressing different aspects of ASD.

When setting up different therapies for your child, engage in interdisciplinary collaboration among professionals from the relevant therapeutic disciplines. For example, if you are incorporating occupational therapy and speech therapy, get an occupational therapist and a speech therapist on board for the best outcomes.

A Holistic Approach

Mental Health Support

In the pursuit of achieving developmental milestones and improving speech and communication, never avoid emotional and mental health aspects. Incorporate therapeutic modalities with advice from the therapist for better emotional regulation, anxiety management, and coping skills.

Nutritional Considerations

For a holistic approach, keep your child's nutritional requirements a priority. While not a replacement for traditional therapies, a balanced diet with added nutritional supplements can positively influence cognitive function and promote well-being.

Mind-Body Practices

Integrate mind-body practices, including mindfulness and relaxation techniques, into the management plan. These practices will aid in managing stress, anxiety, and sensory sensitivities, contributing to a more centered approach to daily life, and back this up by building a solid support network. Although it can take time to set up, you can also connect with other parents facing similar journeys, creating a community where experiences are shared and empathy flows freely.

Furthermore, incorporate sensory-friendly spaces within your home. These spaces offer a calming environment where sensory input is carefully managed. It can also serve as a haven for your child to retreat to when sensory challenges become overwhelming.

Remember, your active involvement throughout the journey is the most influential factor in nurturing your child's mental health and overall development. Your commitment to their emotional well-being creates a foundation for them to thrive.

Tech for Autism Management

Technology can streamline the management of autism when executed correctly. You can easily access tools and resources for communication, learning, and daily functioning for children on the autism spectrum. Here are several aspects of how technology is utilized in autism management:

Communication Apps

Fortunately, technology has brought forth a multitude of Augmentative and Alternative Communication (AAC) apps that can be valuable tools to stimulate your child's communication skills. Think of these apps as personalized communication companions designed especially for your child. These applications assist individuals with limited or no verbal communication abilities. AAC apps often include a variety of symbols, pictures, or text that users can select to convey their thoughts, needs, or feelings.

Likewise, social stories are narrative interventions used to teach social skills and behavior. Social story apps allow for the creation of personalized stories with images and text to help individuals with autism understand and navigate social situations.

Remember, each child is special, and finding the right AAC app may require some research. Be patient, involve your child in the process, and observe which apps align best with their communication preferences.

Educational Apps

When it comes to helping your child learn, there are some really cool educational apps out there. Most of the apps use fun pictures and games to help your child understand letters and words. If your child likes numbers, some apps turn learning numbers into games, kind of like the fun activities in structured play. Just like vocabulary and math apps, you'll also find apps for science, arts, music, and various others to make learning simple and fun. Some examples include Endless Alphabet and iBione-Wetland, but it is always wise to try different apps to see which fit your child best. After all, none of these apps come as one-size-fits-all, and you may need to research more to find the right one for your child.

Assistive Technology Devices

Let's chat about some awesome tools that can really make a difference for your child. Assistive technology devices are special gadgets created to aid your child with different needs, and they can be incredibly helpful in daily life. First off, consider communication apps. These apps turn a tablet into a powerful communication tool.

For some fantastic sensory support, there are devices like noise-canceling headphones or fidget spinners. These little helpers can make the world less overwhelming for your child and promote a sense of calm and control.

Likewise, if your child finds writing challenging, there are devices like speech-to-text tools. They come with digital pens that turn spoken words into written ones, making it easier for your child to express their thoughts. It's a bit like having a writing assistant right at their fingertips. For reading assistance, e-books and audiobooks can be game changers.

Remember, assistive technology devices are there to support your child's needs. Furthermore, these devices can be personalized. So, whether it's communication, sensory support, writing, or reading, there's always a tech tool to make a positive difference.

Wearable Technology

Take smartwatches, for instance. These are like mini-computers on your child's wrist, offering various features, including telling the time, setting reminders, and even tracking physical activity. GPS trackers are another helpful wearable tech. These devices act as silent guardians, ensuring your child's safety and allowing you to keep track of their whereabouts.

Fitness trackers can also be enjoyable additions. These gadgets can help your child stay active and motivated. They turn physical activities into actionable milestones and make moving an enjoyable part of your child's routine.

Remember, wearable technology aims to simplify and enhance your child's life. These wearables can be customized to meet your child's specific needs. Whether it's staying organized, ensuring safety, providing sensory comfort, or promoting physical activity, wearable tech offers options for every aspect of your child's journey.

Virtual Reality (VR) and Augmented Reality (AR)

Imagine VR as a magical portal. When your child puts on VR goggles, it's similar to stepping into a different reality altogether. They can explore new places, meet fascinating characters, or even go on virtual adventures for an immersive experience.

Now, AR is a blend of the real and the virtual, adding digital elements to the real world. With this tech, they can see virtual objects in their own space, turning their surroundings into an interactive playground. Likewise, to promote educational activities, VR can take your child to historical events, outer space, or even inside the human body. The scenarios are endless.

Remember, it's all about balance and age-appropriate content. Thoughtfully introduce VR and AR experiences to make it an enjoyable part of your child's development.

Telehealth Services

Here's another incredible tool that can make accessing healthcare a breeze. Telehealth services can bring the doctor's office to the comfort of your own home through technology.

Imagine being able to connect with healthcare professionals through video calls. Telehealth is just that – a virtual visit to the doctor. You can discuss your child's health, show symptoms, and get advice, all through a computer or phone screen. It's convenient for regular check-ups or consultations with specialists. Furthermore, it eliminates the need for travel, making healthcare more accessible.

Data Collection and Analysis Tools

Technology makes it easy to collect data concerning behaviors and interventions. You can use these data collection tools and digital platforms for recording and analyzing information and sharing it with therapists to track progress, identify patterns, and make informed decisions in the management of autism.

Key Takeaways

- There are lots of different therapies for your child, from ones with studies behind them like ABA and CBT to fun ones like horse riding and music. You can mix them up to find what works best.

- Speech therapy helps your child talk better or use other ways like sign language. Your child will play games and do exercises to get better at communicating.

- Occupational therapy helps with things like holding a pencil or buttoning a shirt. Your child will do activities to get better at daily tasks, making them more independent and confident.

- CBT helps change negative thoughts and behaviors. A trained therapist allows your child to recognize and change these thoughts, making them more positive and constructive.

- AAC aids if your child struggles to communicate. It's a special toolkit for communication, using things like pictures or gestures. Your child works with professionals to find the best way to express themselves.

- Sensory Integration Therapy is like a playful activity that lets your child handle things like sounds or textures. It makes daily activities more accessible for your child.

- The Lovaas Model is about learning new things with the help of ABA principles. It reduces challenging behaviors and teaches valuable skills.

- Physical therapy helps with moving and coordination. Your child will do exercises to improve specific skills.

- Sometimes, medicine is part of the plan. It's not the main thing, but it can help with specific problems like hyperactivity or anxiety.

- Before choosing what to do, it's essential to understand your child's abilities, how they talk and deal with senses, and if other things are going on. Professionals can help with this.

- Focus on what's most important for your child – like talking, making friends, dealing with senses, or doing things on their own. This helps make therapy more targeted and helpful.

- Start with things that directly help what's most important. For example, if talking is a big deal, start with speech therapy. Then, bring in other therapies step by step.

- Remember feelings. Include things like talking about feelings, eating well, and relaxing exercises. Create a support network with other parents going through similar things.
- Use technology to make learning fun. Apps for talking and learning, and even devices that help with sensory issues, can make a big difference. Virtual and augmented reality can also be exciting ways to learn and explore.

Now that you've streamlined every aspect of your child's management plan, the upcoming chapter will touch on topics like self-care and your well-being because it's you who will be playing an active role throughout the journey.

Chapter 8: The Caregiver's Journey

"It's not selfish to love yourself, take care of yourself, and make your happiness a priority. It's necessary." - Mandy Hale.

Think of it like this: if you've ever been on a plane, you'll know how the flight attendants show everyone how to use the oxygen masks in case of an emergency. They always tell you to put on your own mask first before helping others. Sounds logical, right? You'll only be able to help others if you help yourself first. That's the basic principle here. However, when it comes to helping your child, it's so easy to forget to even consider yourself.

Before becoming a parent, it was natural to consider your own needs before anyone else's. It's when you bring life into this world that you learn what it's like to have unconditional love and care for someone else. Every parent loves and cares for their child, even more so if their child has special needs. It makes you feel extra protective and responsible for their wellbeing. However, if you want to take care of your child as best as you can, you first have to take care of yourself, which is easier said than done.

The irony is clear – neglecting self-care leads to burnout, and that benefits no one. Prioritizing self-care isn't selfish; it's a survival strategy for both you and your child on this rollercoaster called parenting. The thing is, there are moments when your child needs you right away, and fitting in self-care becomes nearly impossible. However, being there for someone else almost every second of the day, especially as a caregiver, takes a lot out of you emotionally, mentally, and physically. To keep going strong and be ready for whatever comes your way, you have to make self-care a top priority.

So, it's essential that you don't forget to take care of yourself too. Being a caregiver can be tiring, so make sure to take breaks and do things you enjoy. This not only helps you but also makes the family environment better. You should also form a support group that not only understands what you're going through but can also step in to help out when you need it.

Burnout

Caring for a child with autism or complex needs is undoubtedly rewarding, but it's also an incredibly demanding role that can lead to burnout if not managed effectively. Many parents find themselves unintentionally neglecting their own emotional, physical, and mental well-being in the process, resulting in exhaustion and emotional strain that feels like a rollercoaster ride. Maybe this sounds familiar to you:

You find yourself canceling plans with friends and family regularly. The once vibrant social life you had becomes a distant memory as you face the daily ups and downs of caring for your child. Weekends that used to be filled with hobbies and relaxation are now consumed by the constant demands of caregiving.

And babysitters? They become a far-fetched dream. The idea of entrusting someone else with the intricate care your child requires becomes increasingly impossible, leaving you with little to no time for self-care or even a simple date night.

Personal appointments, like visits to the doctor or dentist, take a backseat. Your focus is primarily on your child's needs, often at the expense of your own health. The sleep you get is either limited or of poor quality as you navigate the nighttime routines and potential disruptions that often accompany the care of a child with special needs.

As the days blend together, you may start feeling emotionally numb, resentful, or cynical towards others. The once joyful and fulfilling role of caregiving transforms into a constant battle, leaving you exhausted, irritable, and struggling to concentrate on even the simplest tasks.

Acknowledging burnout is a crucial step for caregivers. It's a signal to reassess priorities, seek support, and reintroduce self-care practices into daily life. Understanding that your well-being is intertwined with your ability to provide quality care is the first step toward preventing negative outcomes and fostering a healthier, more sustainable caregiving journey.

Financial Strain

Caring for a child with autism involves juggling many roles, from coordinating appointments with behavioral therapists, occupational therapists, and speech therapists to researching additional management strategies like music or recreation therapy. Managing these appointments can be extremely challenging, especially when you try to synchronize them with your own demanding work schedules and the needs of your other children.

The worst part is that this struggle doesn't end with scheduling difficulties. There's also the added financial burden that often accompanies these management strategies. Parents are caught in a web of uncertainty, questioning what they should independently pay for and what is covered by insurance or school programs. It's a puzzle that adds stress to an already overwhelming situation, and many families grapple with the financial strain of navigating through the array of management strategies tailored to their child's unique needs.

Mothers, in particular, often take on the role of a "case manager," tirelessly advocating for their child with autism spectrum disorder (ASD). Unfortunately, this advocacy often comes at a cost to their own careers. So, not only do you suffer from emotional burnout, but you also have to deal with the stress of managing the added financial burden this condition brings.

There is nothing worse than having to worry about money while also dealing with your child's special needs and health issues. In the midst of these financial and scheduling challenges, burnout becomes an all-too-common companion for parents. The emotional, physical, and financial toll can be overwhelming, which is why it is so important that you recognize the signs of burnout and prioritize your well-being.

Self-Care for the Caregiver

You cannot pour anything out of an empty cup. Prioritizing self-care is not a selfish act; instead, it is a fundamental necessity when it comes to caring for your child and your entire family. By ensuring your own well-being, you are sustaining your ability to meet the demands of caregiving and creating a foundation for a healthier and more supportive family environment. Remember, your capacity to care for others is deeply connected to how well you take care of yourself. So, start taking care of yourself today before you become too exhausted to take care of anyone else. Here are some steps you can take to help you get started.

1. Seek Help

Asking for help can be tough, especially if you're used to shouldering the burden by yourself. However, this is the first and the most crucial step of your self-care journey. First, you have to figure out exactly where you need help and who could provide that help, and then, there's the tricky part of asking for it. You might have people around you who are willing to help, but they might not know you're struggling or how to pitch in.

Maybe your friend genuinely wants to help you but isn't a mind-reader. They might not know you're drowning in tasks or what would make a real difference. So, it's not just about asking for help; it's about being clear about what you need. Now, here's the emotional hurdle – asking for help is humbling. It's admitting that you can't do it all on your own, showing a bit of vulnerability, and trusting others with some of your caregiving responsibilities. Accepting help when it's offered can be even harder.

For instance, your neighbor sees you're stressed and offers to lend a hand. Taking them up on it doesn't mean you're weak or failing as a caregiver. It shows you're smart enough to know when you need support and humble enough to take it when it's there. So, next time someone extends a helping hand, don't overthink it – grab it. It's not a sign of weakness; it's a smart move to make your caregiving journey a bit smoother.

2. Find Your Support System

Once you've gathered the courage to ask for help, the second step comes into play – finding your support system. Raising a child takes a village, especially if your child needs extra support. This village can include family, friends, and even professionals who play a crucial role in both your life and your child's.

Your child has unique needs, and navigating a world not designed for them can be challenging. Many children with autism benefit from various types of therapy to learn the skills necessary for this journey. It's like handing them a set of tools to navigate their singular path in life. In fact, caregivers, too, often find themselves in need of professional guidance. Life throws curveballs, and you might need someone to help you navigate through tough times.

For instance, consider you're struggling to communicate effectively with your child, and it's taking a toll on both of you. This is where a speech therapist can step in and offer strategies to enhance communication. It's not just about the child – these sessions can equip you, the caregiver, with tools to better connect with and understand your child.

And don't forget the power of your personal support squad. Your family and friends can be the backbone of your village. They're the ones who can provide that listening ear, share a laugh, or simply be there when things get tough. Maybe you have a friend or sibling who's been through similar challenges. Their advice and empathy will be invaluable.

3. Take a Break

Managing stress levels and taking care of yourself is a bit like running a marathon. It requires endurance, but even the most seasoned runners need to catch their breath. For parents and caregivers, especially those caring for children with autism or complex needs, the journey can be particularly challenging. Picture this: You've been managing back-to-back appointments, dealing with daily challenges, and juggling various responsibilities. It's tough, right? That's why it's crucial to show yourself some grace and embrace the concept of taking a break.

This might mean allowing yourself an hour to unwind, whether it's reading a book, going for a walk, or simply enjoying a cup of tea in peace. Consider it a vital recharge for both your mental and emotional well-being. Now, here's where respite care comes into play – it's not just a luxury; it's a necessity. Get the help of a trusted friend, family member, or professional caregiver to step in for a while. This break can provide you with the time you need to rest and recoup, ensuring you return to your caregiving role with renewed energy and resilience.

In the whirlwind of caregiving, finding moments of peace can feel like a rarity. That's where journaling, gratitude practice, and affirmations come in as powerful tools. Consider this scenario: You've had a particularly challenging day, and it feels like the weight of the world is on your shoulders. Journaling provides an outlet for these emotions. Take a few minutes to jot down your thoughts, frustrations, and even victories. It's a therapeutic way to release pent-up emotions and gain clarity.

Now, let's talk about gratitude practice. In the midst of chaos, finding things to be grateful for might seem daunting, but it's surprisingly effective. Try noting down three things you're thankful for each day – it could be a small achievement, a supportive friend, or even a moment of peace. This practice can shift your focus from challenges to positive aspects of your life, fostering a more optimistic outlook.

Affirmations, too, play a significant role. Picture this: You're feeling overwhelmed, and self-doubt is creeping in. That's when affirmations come to the rescue. Create positive statements about your capabilities and resilience. Repeat them, believe them, and let them serve as a reminder of your strength. It's a small yet impactful way to cultivate a more positive mindset amidst the demands of caregiving.

4. Prioritize Time with Your Partner and Family

Think of your family as a team, where everyone has their role. When you're busy caring for a special needs child, it's easy to get caught up in everything that must be done. Now, if you have other kids in the family, they might be feeling a bit left out, or they're not getting as much attention.

Here's a simple way to look at it: Your caregiving responsibilities can be like a big puzzle, and each family member is a piece of that puzzle. If you spend all your time on one piece, the others might feel a bit neglected.

Now, think about spending some quality time with your partner and other kids. It doesn't have to be anything fancy – maybe it's playing a game, having a little chat, or doing something fun together. When you do this, you'll be giving attention to all the pieces of the puzzle. It helps everyone feel valued and included.

Remember, your other kids might be feeling a mix of emotions – maybe a bit left out or wondering why things are different now. By making time for them, you're not just taking care of yourself, but you're also showing them that they're an important part of the family. It's like making sure all the puzzle pieces fit together, creating a happy and balanced family picture.

5. Set Priorities

You've probably got a to-do list that feels a mile long. Work demands, household chores, and, of course, your child's complex needs. It's a lot to handle. Now, let's zoom in on your priorities. Decide which tasks are the VIPs of your day. You've got to include yourself on that list. It's not being selfish; it's about being smart.

Consider this: You've got a big work project, your child's therapy sessions, and a friend asking for a favor. If you treat all of these as equally urgent, you'll burn yourself out. But if you make a clear list of priorities, giving yourself a slot is like having a well-organized toolbox. You can grab the right tool at the right time, making everything run smoother.

Self-care is not just about spa days (though those are great, too!). It's about the basics – taking a breather when you need it, getting enough sleep, doing something that makes you happy, essentially just treating yourself like a priority. This includes knowing when to say no. By knowing your limits and saying no when needed, you're the boss of your own circus.

6. Find Purpose Outside of Caregiving

Being a caregiver is a big part of your life, but it's not the only part. Think of it as your favorite book – caregiving might be a significant chapter, but the whole story has many more pages. You are more than just a caregiver. Knowing what else makes you happy, what fills your cup, is vital.

Here's a challenge for you: Complete this sentence – "I am a caregiver AND..." If you're finding it tricky to finish that sentence, it's time for a bit of soul-searching. Maybe you used to love painting, but it got pushed to the side when caregiving took center stage. Reconnecting with your artistic side could be the "AND" in your sentence. It's not about adding more to your plate; it's about rediscovering what brings you joy and fulfillment.

So, take a moment to reflect, think about what used to make your heart sing, and let that be a part of your story. You're not just a caregiver; you're a multi-faceted, unique individual with passions and interests waiting to be rediscovered.

7. Practice Mindfulness/Relaxation Techniques

Taking a moment to unwind is like hitting the reset button for your mind and body. Here are some relaxation techniques with some easy-to-follow resources.

Deep Breathing Technique

1. Find a comfortable seat or lie down.
2. Close your eyes and take a deep breath through your nose, counting to four.
3. Hold your breath for a count of four.
4. Exhale slowly through your mouth for a count of four.
5. Repeat for several breath cycles.

Guided Meditation

1. Choose a quiet space to sit or lie down.
2. Use meditation apps or online videos that guide you through calming visualizations or mindfulness exercises.
3. Focus on your breath or a soothing voice guiding you through relaxation.

Yoga

1. Find a quiet spot with a yoga mat or comfortable surface.
2. Follow online yoga sessions or use beginner-friendly apps.
3. Start with gentle stretches and poses, focusing on your breath and body awareness.

Music Therapy

1. Create a playlist of your favorite calming tunes.
2. Find a comfortable space to listen, whether sitting or lying down.
3. Let the music wash over you, paying attention to the melodies and rhythms.

Mindful Walking

1. Step outside and take a leisurely walk.
2. Pay attention to each step, the sensation of your feet on the ground, and the sounds around you.
3. Focus on your breath and the movement of your body.

Meditative Hot Bath

1. Run a warm bath with your favorite calming scents (lavender, chamomile, etc.).
2. Dim the lights and create a soothing atmosphere.
3. As you soak, let your mind relax and enjoy the warmth.

Remember, the key is consistency. Make these practices a regular part of your routine. If you're unsure where to start, many online platforms offer beginner-friendly sessions. Whether it's a few minutes of deep breathing or a longer yoga session, finding what resonates with you is the key to making these techniques effective in promoting relaxation and mindfulness in your daily life.

Key Takeaways

- Prioritizing self-care is essential for you as a caregiver and a parent of a child with special needs.

- Neglecting self-care can lead to burnout, affecting both you and your child's well-being.

- Asking for and accepting help is crucial for you, even though it can be challenging and humbling.

- Building a support system of friends, family, and professionals can provide invaluable assistance to you.

- Taking regular breaks and engaging in activities you enjoy is vital for you to recharge and maintain your resilience.

- Identifying priorities and setting boundaries helps prevent overwhelm for you and ensures self-care remains a priority.

- Exploring interests and finding purpose outside of caregiving contributes to your overall well-being.

- Practicing relaxation techniques like deep breathing, meditation, yoga, and mindful activities promotes mental and emotional balance.

Remember, parenting a child with autism is a journey that requires strength, resilience, and a network of support. Taking care of yourself is not a luxury but a necessity. By acknowledging that you're not alone, seeking support, and prioritizing your well-being, you equip yourself to be a more effective and compassionate caregiver for your child. In fostering a supportive environment, both you and your child can thrive together.

Chapter 9: Educational Empowerment

"Adapting our own perception, following rather than leading, and building bridges are all keys to helping the child with autism learn." - Adele Devine

Your child's education plays a crucial role in their growth and development. Parents of children with autism often struggle to provide their children with much-needed educational empowerment. If you're facing similar challenges, this chapter will give you and your child the tools you need to find a supportive environment where they can learn crucial skills and build on existing strengths. You'll also learn about navigating the special needs education system, along with the rights you and your child with autism have regarding their education.

Leveraging Special Education Services

Since they tend to develop repetitive behaviors, children with autism often take special interest in activities involving repetition. Leveraging your child's intense interest in a particular activity, subject, or task is crucial for their educational empowerment. These interests can help your child build skills that they would struggle to develop without a motivating foundation to build on.

While they might seem like a hobby or enjoyable activity to neurotypical individuals, for people on the autism spectrum, special interest areas (SIA) are a crucial part of life; in fact, sometimes, these are the only points of reference or ways for children with autism to interact with the outside world. These areas can vary from one child with autism to another. For example, some might be interested in music or a specific instrument, others in history. Some children with autism become fascinated with puzzles or activities involving organizational skills.

It's also crucial to emphasize that children express their interest in SIA differently. For example, of two children who like memorizing things, one might excel in recalling long lists, and the other is better at remembering pictures and associating them with specific contexts. Either way, if there is one thing in particular that captures your child's interest, and they can study it, they can create a world where they'll always have something familiar to turn to and function and grow without fearing the unknown.

The Role of SIA in Social, Communication, and Behavior Improvement

Leveraging SIAs positively impacts children with autism. By letting your child speak to you about their special interests (or having them communicate with you through other means), you're helping them to work on their social, emotional, communication, and behavior skills.

Boosting Self-Image

Due to their numerous challenges, children with autism often have a negative self-image. However, when they engage in or communicate about their special interests, they get an unparalleled confidence boost. They become motivated to express themselves and begin to feel accepted and connected to others. Moreover, they can use their special interests to connect with others who have the same interests and are facing similar challenges (whether due to autism or another condition).

Improved Self-Regulation

When they can share or participate in their interests, they're filled with positive emotions like pride, happiness, and enthusiasm. If your child struggles with identifying, understanding, conveying, and regulating emotions, every opportunity you can take to help them overcome this challenge is welcome. Since SIAs are an enjoyable activity for neurodivergent children, they can use these to calm themselves when big emotions threaten to take control. For example, some children on the spectrum like listening to music or solving puzzles when upset, using this activity as a self-regulation tool.

Better Communication Skills

SIAs can also motivate your child to improve their communication skills. Children with autism often speak in a monotone or unusual voice. However, when allowed to share their special interests, they'll switch to different speech patterns, clearly emphasizing crucial words and conveying enthusiasm with their tone of voice, gestures, or whatever communication method they prefer. For verbally autistic children, the more they can speak about their interests, the more their vocabulary, word order, and syntax will improve. With question-and-answer sessions, communication broadens. When explaining something familiar, talking about it feels natural, so they won't be anxious about how their responses will be received.

Improved Fine Motor Skills

Another benefit your child can gain from leveraging SIAs is an improvement of their fine motor skills. Children with autism can be clumsy because they can't move their bodies in the same fluid way their neurotypical peers do. Plenty of special interests help develop fine motor skills, from making art to playing computer games.

Better Sensory Tolerance

When engaged in a special interest, a child with autism is less likely to be triggered by any surrounding sensory stimuli because of their ability to hyper-focus on the task at hand. At the same time, crucial skills are being developed as a byproduct. For example, if smells easily trigger your child, and their SIA involves animals, they might be able to build up a tolerance for strong smells if the animals they play with are the source of odors.

Implementing Special Interests in the Child's Education

The first step in helping children leverage their special interests is finding what sparks their interest. Then, it can be integrated into the educational planning. Next, you can start applying the child's interests to your communication, incorporating the vocabulary into teachable moments at home and teaching areas at school. For example, if your child is interested in cats, they can be encouraged to read books and find as much information as they can about these animals, then share what they learned with others.

Keep in mind that your child's special interest can change over time, so make sure that you and their teachers regularly update the interest list. Monitor your child's interest to see whether they're still engaging in the same activities and ask your child's teachers to stay up to date with your child's performance in the tasks they get related to their special interests.

As your child can have multiple SIAs at a time, make sure to switch them up regularly, as relying only on one during their education can reduce its effectiveness. It makes the child feel like you or the teachers aren't interested in their other interests and are pressured to perform well in only one, neither of which is conducive to building trust and laying the foundation for an empowering educational experience. Even if your child prefers some activities more than others, the less preferred ones can still be good motivators to keep their interest in a broader range. After all, the more interests they have, the more topics they have to talk about or otherwise communicate about confidently, the more ways they'll have to express their feelings and thoughts, and the more connected they'll be to others. When implementing SIAs in their child's education, it's fundamental to develop a plan that utilizes their interests in learning new skills in a way that works best for the child.

Special Education 101

At its core, special education aims to meet the individual needs of children with different forms of disabilities. This is a unique (and free) form of instruction that can be provided at the individual's home, in a traditional classroom, or in another environment that suits the purpose. Beyond catering to the children's wants and needs, special education has the purpose of conveying special needs children the same information their neurotypical peers are also learning at school.

There are numerous educational opportunities for autistic students, from general education classrooms and classrooms enriched with resources for specific needs through special education classrooms to fully inclusive settings where children with autism can learn along with their non-autistic peers. Depending on their needs, some children on the spectrum can only thrive in educational settings specifically tailored to their needs. Others do well in autistic-only settings where they can interact with other children with autism and different abilities.

In the US and the UK, special education is governed by federal laws that ensure all children with disabilities can receive the support they need during their educational journey. The Individuals with Disabilities Education Act (US) is the primary law authorizing special education for children with disabilities while also granting early intervention services that parents of infants and preschoolers with disabilities can take advantage of in different states. Meanwhile, Section 504 of the Rehabilitation Act of 1973 (US) prevents all publicly or privately funded programs in schools from discriminating against children based on disabilities. Under this law, a person with a disability is someone with a physical or mental condition that substantially restricts them in their activities and has proof of their limitations. Naturally, children with autism fall under Individuals with Disabilities Education Act definition of "children with disabilities" and, therefore, are eligible to receive special education and related services.

Parents' Participation in Special Needs Education

Whether your child goes to public school or is enrolled in a private special needs program, you, as a parent, need to be tightly involved and advocate for your child's rights and needs. Your relationship with the school will make an outstanding difference in your child's education. However, for this to happen, you should be fully informed about your own rights during the process of special education. Here are a few things to keep in mind when it comes to your involvement in your child's education:

- Your child's schools must inform you of your rights as a parent and your child's rights.

- Your child's school must obtain your written consent to evaluate your child's disability.

- You have the right to demand that your child's file in the educational institution remain confidential.

- You have the right to disagree with any action and decision made by your child's school regarding the classroom or environment in which they receive their education and request the necessary changes.

- You have the right to become a member of the team that aims to determine your child's special needs and interests education services the school will provide to meet these needs, and the location where your child will receive their education.

Developing the IEP

One of the most decisive steps in planning your child's educational path is developing their Individualized Educational Plan (IEP). This is a collaborative approach between all the team members involved in supporting your child. When devising an IEP, the following areas must be considered.

The Child's Interests and Strengths

Your child's interests and strengths form the foundation for strategizing a continued educational program. The team's goal is to build new skills and behaviors based on the child's strengths. For example, suppose a child has a specific area or subject they excel in. In that case, they should be encouraged to continue developing and showcasing their skills in this area/subject in front of their peers, encouraging socialization and building confidence.

The Parent's Main Concerns Regarding the Child's Education

Make sure you express your concerns related to your child's education to the IEP team. For example, if you're concerned that your child is facing discrimination due to their disabilities, voicing your concerns will help the IEP take the necessary steps to address them. Any issue that may impact your child's education should be considered and resolved by the IEP team.

The Results of the Child's Most Recent Evaluation

Since your child's needs and abilities will change over time, they should be continuously evaluated by the IEP team. The most recent comprehensive evaluation (typically done before establishing the initial IEP plan and then three years into it) should greatly impact your child's educational plan. It shows the IEP team the child's current and evolving strengths and abilities, which the team can continue to build on in the future.

The Child's Academic, Functional, and Developmental Needs

The IEP team must also include in their planning your child's progress towards the current academic goals, state assessment results, report cards, the effectiveness of the current educational plan, and eventual modification to improve it. They should also consider any functional or developmental needs that might have arisen recently and may affect the child's everyday life.

Other Factors

Additional factors your child's IEP must consider are behaviors that might affect the child's learning capabilities or might be disruptive to other children, the child's language skills, visual or hearing impairment, need for assistive technological devices, and any other communication needs.

As a general rule of thumb, assistive technological services and devices should be considered for any child who needs an Individualized Educational Plan. In children with autism (verbal and nonverbal), communication represents a considerable obstacle, which assistive devices can help surmount. If it is determined that your child needs these services, this should be included in their IEP (in a written or otherwise easily accessible form so the parents can have proof of it).

Suppose your child is transferred to another school or school district. In that case, they should be able to transfer their Individualized Educational Plan, along with the requirement for assistive technological services and devices.

Advocacy and Rights

Beyond their legal right to free and appropriate education granted by the IDEA, children with autism also enjoy other forms of protection during their education. By advocating for all their rights, you can ensure your child's needs are met at all times. Below are some of the most common rights of children with special needs.

Right to Least Restrictive Environment

As per the IDEA, your child has the right to receive their education in the "least restrictive environment" (LRE). In other words, they should be placed in an environment where they can interact with their neurotypical peers during the process known as inclusion. In public schools, this is often achieved by providing a child with one-on-one aid, who accompanies them and helps them navigate the school day while they receive the general educational curriculum, so the child doesn't have to feel isolated or inadequate. Naturally, LRE will not be appropriate for all children with autism, but should definitely be in the mix for consideration.

Right to Early Intervention Services

Early intervention services (EI) are statewide programs funded through the IDEA federal grants. They can be granted to children (under the age of three) with any form of developmental delay at no cost. Early intervention services aim to address the child's needs and aren't limited to services available in the child's residential area. The services are determined by the Individual Family Service Plan (IFSP), which is created after a comprehensive evaluation, skills assessment, and potential mapping. EI services might include physical therapy, speech and language therapy, regular psychological evaluation, occupational therapy, and more.

Right to Special Education Services

Once the early intervention services are terminated, the next step is the right to access special education services provided by your local school district. It focuses on providing educational empowerment based on an Individualized Education Program (IEP). To obtain these services, contact your school district. Your child will have to go through an evaluation of their developmental state, speech and language skills, behavioral assessment, evaluation of their adaptive skills, and an unstructured diagnostic play session. You will be interviewed as well.

Right to Extended School Year Services

If your child falls behind in their education during school breaks, they might be entitled to extended school year services (ESY). This way, your child can receive instructions during long breaks (for example, during the summer break) to prevent regression. This is particularly important during the beginning of your child's educational path, as any regression can impact their future learning ability both mentally and psychologically.

Rights to Assistive Technology

As mentioned earlier, access to assistive technology can serve as a pathway for children with autism to access the general education curriculum and a fantastic way to improve functional life skills. The assistive technology and accompanying services are provided by the school district, and lack of availability or high costs shouldn't be used as an excuse for denying your child access to the devices or services. The same applies to a lack of adequate teacher training. Moreover, training the child and the teacher's aides to use the devices can be listed in the child's IEP as assistive technology services, which means the costs will be covered by the federal grant. Your child should be allowed to take an assistive device home if having the device available 24/7 helps them stay on track with their educational goals. You, as a parent, have a right to disagree with the school's decision regarding the eligibility or use of assistive technological services and devices. If you disagree with the school's evaluation, you have the right to demand another independent assessment of your child's needs at the school district's expense. Any difference between the school's initial and an independent evaluation should be resolved by the child's IEP team.

Key Takeaways

- Since special interests are a hallmark of ASD, leveraging them throughout the child's education is the best way to give the right tools for a fulfilling life.

- Engaging in special interests helps children build confidence and improves their social, behavioral, cognitive, and other functional life skills.

- Children with autism will also benefit from developing an Individualized Education Program (IEP), which is a collaboration between parents, teachers, therapists, and other professionals.

- Children with autism have the right to free and appropriate public education in the least restrictive environment (receiving instructions along with neurotypical children).

- Besides the right to early intervention services until the age of three, children with autism also have a right to special education services, which can be obtained at your local school district when your child starts their early education after the age of three.

- Depending on needs and capabilities, your child might also qualify for the use of assistive technological devices and services, which are also provided by the school district.

- Beyond knowing their rights, it's also crucial for you to familiarize yourself with how the special needs education system works and what resources might be available to your child.

The next, final chapter explores the challenges and joys of raising a child with Autism Spectrum Disorder, providing additional guidance for parents to help meet their child's needs along with their own.

Chapter 10: Unique Challenges and Joys

"To be yourself in a world that is constantly trying to make you something else is the greatest accomplishment." - Ralph Waldo Emerson.

In a world that often misunderstands the vast spectrum of neurodiversity, many well-intentioned folk consider neurodivergent individuals incapable of being good parents. Stereotypes and misconceptions have often painted a picture of incapability, overshadowing the incredible strengths and different perspectives that autistic individuals bring to the table when it comes to parenting. However, it's high time these myths get dispelled. Autistic individuals can be exceptional parents, and their neurodivergent edge can make them extraordinarily wonderful players in the journey of raising children.

Parenting, by its very nature, is a multifaceted experience that demands adaptability, patience, and an understanding of a child's diverse needs. Autistic parents possess qualities that, when embraced, can enhance the parenting experience, taking it to new heights. Yes, challenges may arise, but with the right strategies and an acceptance of one's neurodivergent identity, autistic parents can navigate parenthood with resilience and ingenuity.

Maybe your meticulous attention to detail will transform everyday routines into structured, enriching experiences for your child. Or maybe it'll be your ability to focus that will create especially engaging and educational environments. As an autistic individual, you'll understand sensory challenges far better than a neurotypical person. This will be especially helpful if your child, like you, is on the autism spectrum.

Society may question the ability of autistic parents to connect emotionally with their children, but reality often tells a different story. Autistic parents, guided by their deep empathy and genuine love, develop strong bonds with their children, fostering an environment of trust and acceptance. The idea that autistic individuals lack emotional connection is a stereotype that crumbles in the face of countless heartfelt moments and shared joys within neurodivergent families.

While the journey may require additional effort, the rewards are immeasurable. Autistic parents possess a reservoir of strength, resilience, and creativity that, when tapped into, transforms the parenting experience. The key lies in embracing one's neurodivergent identity, acknowledging the challenges, and uncovering the advantages that come with being an autistic parent.

Autism and Parenting

When considering the prospect of autistic parents having children, a common question that arises is whether there's a high chance of their children being on the autism spectrum. However, contrary to some misconceptions, research indicates that the risk of having an child with autism is not notably higher when both parents are on the autism spectrum. In fact, the majority of children with autism are born to parents who are not themselves diagnosed as autistic.

However, when one parent is on the spectrum, there may be a slightly increased likelihood that their child could exhibit certain behaviors associated with autism. These may include challenges related to social communication or sensory processing. However, this increased likelihood does not guarantee that your child will be autistic, as the interplay of genetics is complex, and each individual is unique.

In the case that your child is indeed on the autism spectrum, that doesn't necessarily have to be a bad thing. In fact, as an autistic parent, you will understand better than anyone else what it's like growing up and experiencing everything that comes with being autistic. Who better than you to guide your child through the intricacies of a heightened sensitivity to sensory stimuli or an inability to make eye contact? You will be able to draw from your own experiences and implement sensory-friendly strategies at home, creating an environment that caters to your child's specific needs. This adaptation is not a result of your autism being a hindrance but rather a demonstration of your ability to use your personal insights to make sure your child feels secure, loved, and flourishes.

In the case that your child is not on the autism spectrum, you can still be a great parent to them. Every child, regardless of their parents' neurodivergent status, is an individual with their own strengths and challenges. It's crucial to approach parenting with an open mind, recognizing and celebrating the diversity within families. Autistic parents can create environments that accommodate their children's needs while nurturing their individuality, just like any neurotypical individual could.

Sensory Needs

Being a parent is an adventure filled with laughter, surprises, and, sometimes, a whole lot of noise. For autistic parents, this journey may come with challenges, particularly when it comes to sensory issues.

Imagine a cozy afternoon at home. Your child, bursting with creativity, decides to explore their musical talents by playing a toy xylophone with great enthusiasm. The sounds reverberate through the room, each note hitting a different pitch. Now, for many parents, this is just a part of the joyful chaos of childhood. But for an autistic parent, the cacophony of unpredictable sounds can be overwhelming. The constant auditory stimulation might trigger discomfort, making it challenging to stay engaged.

In another scenario, picture a lovely day outside. The sun is shining, and your child is eager to embrace the outdoors. However, as a parent on the autism spectrum, the sensation of the sun's warmth, the breeze against the skin, and the various textures underfoot may be intensified. While the child gleefully runs around, you might find it challenging to manage the sensory overload, leading to a potential meltdown or withdrawal.

Or, consider the heartwarming moment when your child rushes to greet you when you return home. The excitement is palpable as the child, filled with joy, wants nothing more than to share that enthusiasm through a tight, affectionate hug. However, for someone with sensory overload, this intense physical contact might trigger discomfort due to heightened sensitivity to touch.

In these everyday scenarios, the clash between the unpredictable sensory demands of parenting and the sensitivities of autism can create moments of tension. An overload of noise, touch, or even the rapid transitions between activities can push an autistic parent to the brink of a sensory meltdown or shutdown.

However, it's crucial to emphasize that this doesn't diminish the love or dedication an autistic parent has for their child. Instead, it highlights the need for understanding and finding adaptive strategies. This might involve creating sensory-friendly spaces at home, or establishing clear routines to provide a sense of predictability. By acknowledging and addressing these challenges, you can create an environment that nurtures both your sensory needs and the unique connection you share with your children.

Handling Sensory Challenges

Handling sensory challenges is certainly an ongoing journey for autistic parents. However, finding effective strategies can greatly enhance your parenting experience. Here are some tips to manage sensory overload:

- **Create Sensory-Friendly Spaces**

Designate specific areas in your home as sensory-friendly zones. These spaces can be dimly lit, with furnishing in soft textures, and have minimal auditory distractions, providing a retreat for both you and your child when needed.

- **Plan Outdoor Activities Strategically**

Take advantage of outdoor play during times when sensory conditions are favorable. A quiet park in the early morning or late afternoon can offer a serene environment for both you and your child to enjoy nature without overwhelming sensory inputs.

- **Establish Quiet Time in the Morning**

Wake up a bit earlier than the rest of the household to have quiet time for personal recharge. Use this time for self-care activities, meditation, or any calming routine that sets a positive tone for the day.

- **Scheduled Breaks for Self-Regulation**

Incorporate short breaks into your daily routine that align with your family's schedule. During these breaks, engage in activities that help regulate your sensory system, like deep breathing exercises, stretching, or a brief moment of solitude.

- **Teach Consent Using Sensory Cues**

Use sensory experiences to teach your child about consent. Establish a communication system where you can express, with kindness, when you need a sensory break. Likewise, encourage your child to communicate their comfort levels so you build mutual respect and awareness of sensory boundaries.

- **Explore Sensory-Friendly Tools**

Introduce sensory-friendly tools, like fidget toys or textured objects, that can provide comfort during overwhelming moments. These tools can serve as a tactile outlet for both you and your child, promoting self-regulation.

Remember, these tips are not one-size-fits-all, and it may take some trial and error to find what works best for you and your family. The key is to create an environment that accommodates sensory needs while fostering positive connections with your children.

Empathy and Emotional Challenges

Empathy is something many autistic parents have, contrary to the common myth that strongly suggests otherwise. While they might express empathy differently toward neurotypical individuals, autistic parents feel emotions intensely and possess a keen sensitivity to the feelings of others.

For instance, consider a scenario where a child starts to show signs of distress through subtle changes in behavior or body language. An autistic parent will be more attuned to these nuances and will be able to pick up the emotional shift and intervene proactively to prevent potential meltdowns.

Autistic individuals often face unique challenges and experiences of feeling misunderstood, under-appreciated, or belittled in a neurotypical world. This shared understanding of struggle contributes to the development of deep empathy.

Autistic parents, having navigated childhood and young adulthood in a world that may not fully embrace neurodiversity, often carry the weight of their own traumas. This shared experience of pain allows them to empathize profoundly with their children's struggles.

Imagine a child, whether neurodivergent or not, feeling left out or overwhelmed in a social situation. An autistic parent, intimately familiar with these emotions, can connect on a profound level. They offer guidance with a blend of love and compassion, drawing from their own experiences of having had to go through similar challenges.

Autistic parents, equipped with an intrinsic understanding of the emotional landscape, excel in guiding their children through difficult moments. Whether it's helping a child cope with sensory overload or navigate social complexities, the empathetic insight of an autistic parent shines through.

The empathetic strength of autistic parents lies in their ability to create a safe and understanding space for their children. This safe haven allows children, whether neurodivergent or neurotypical, to express their feelings without fear of judgment, fostering a bond built on shared experiences and genuine compassion.

Embracing Your Identity

Being an autistic parent means doing things a bit differently from what people might expect. Maybe you like to stick to a tight schedule or prefer not to have too many kids over for playtime. Taking some quiet time away from the kids in the afternoons might be your thing, and your kids might have fewer activities during the week.

But here's the thing – it doesn't mean you're a bad parent. Autistic parents love their kids just like any other parent. You've figured out a system that works for your family, meeting everyone's needs in your particular way.

Parenting, though, comes with a bunch of unwritten rules, and there's this fear of being judged if you don't follow them. Even though everyone knows that one-size-fits-all parenting isn't really a thing, if you're an autistic parent doing things a bit differently, you might get some negative attention from others.

Sometimes, even if no one says anything out loud, you could feel you're breaking all the supposed parenting rules. This feeling of not doing things the "normal" way can bring shame, and that's tough to deal with – coming from both inside yourself and from what you think others might be thinking.

The point to remember is that your way of parenting, with all its quirks and differences, is what makes your family work. You're not alone in finding your own path, and there's strength in embracing your identity as an autistic parent, regardless of what society might expect.

Dealing with Shame

Dealing with shame can be a tough nut to crack, but some strategies might help you navigate those challenging moments. Here are some tips for handling shame:

- **Practice Self-Compassion**

Treat yourself with kindness and understanding, especially when you find parenting difficult and exhausting. Instead of being too hard on yourself, treat yourself with the same comfort and support you would give to your child when they're going through a tough time.

- **Remember You're Not Alone**

Recognize that many parents, both autistic and neurotypical, face similar struggles. Knowing that you're not alone in your experiences can help reduce feelings of isolation and shame.

- **Cultivate Mindfulness**

Practice mindfulness to stay present in the moment and avoid being overwhelmed by negative feelings. Mindfulness techniques, such as deep breathing or grounding exercises, can help you maintain an even keel amidst difficult emotions.

- **Radical Self-Acceptance**

Embrace radical self-acceptance, acknowledging and accepting yourself exactly as you are. Work with a therapist if you need to. They can give you valuable support in this journey. Identify and celebrate what makes you a great parent, and trust your instincts when it comes to understanding your child.

- **Lean into Your Strengths**

Trust your strengths as an autistic parent. Recognize that some conventional rules won't apply to your family, and that's perfectly okay. Lean into your abilities, such as heightened awareness of your home environment, and appreciate the insights your autism brings to your parenting style.

Remember, embracing your identity as an autistic parent means accepting yourself, quirks and all. You look at life from a different angle and have a set of strengths that make you an outstanding parent, and there is no shame in that.

Building a Support Network

Building a support system is crucial for any parent, and for autistic parents, it can make a significant difference in navigating the challenges of raising children. Unfortunately, due to the stigma and discrimination surrounding autism, many autistic parents find themselves lacking the support they truly need. Here are some insights and tips for handling the lack of support systems:

Autistic parents may feel out of place in conventional social spaces like 'mommy groups,' often designed without neurodivergent perspectives in mind. Plus, the tendency to have a smaller circle of very close friends rather than a wide network can limit available support options.

Autistic parents might have fewer neurodivergent friends who can provide support, as their friends may also be seeking support for themselves. The limited options for support can lead to exhaustion, making it essential to explore alternative strategies.

Finding Help

- **Allocate Resources Wisely**

Keep a little room in your budget for support services, ensuring you have the means to address tasks that can be energy-draining. This allocation helps prevent your reserves from getting depleted, leaving you with more energy for meaningful interactions with your child.

- **Connect with Fellow Parents on the Autism Spectrum**

Parenting as an autistic individual brings unique challenges, and reaching out to others who share this experience can offer a sense of validation, empathy, and practical support. Joining communities or networks specifically designed for parents on the autism spectrum creates a space where shared experiences become a source of strength.

- **Identify a Parenting Mentor**

Look for a mentor within your circle – a relative, friend, or someone from your club or church whose parenting style you respect. A parenting mentor can serve as a role model, offering a listening ear and valuable advice based on their own experiences.

- **Explore Professional Help for Family Communication**

Consider seeking professional assistance for family communication dynamics, including parent-child and partner interactions. Individual or family therapy can provide a platform to identify challenges and collaboratively develop effective solutions. Therapy is not about "curing" autism but about finding practical ways to manage the unique challenges of living on the autism spectrum.

- **Engage an Advocate for Communication with Professionals**

Having an advocate can be invaluable when communicating with schools, doctors, and other professionals. An advocate can help ensure that your needs and concerns are effectively conveyed, fostering a collaborative and supportive environment.

- **Enroll in a Parenting Class or Course**

Participating in a parenting class offers valuable skills in various areas, including insights into the often unspoken "rules" of parenting. These courses provide practical knowledge and strategies to enhance your parenting journey.

- **Prioritize Personal Recharge Time**

Finding moments for personal recharge is essential. Building in time for self-care and relaxation helps maintain a balance between your responsibilities as a parent and your own well-being.

- **Incorporate Structure and Routine**

Establishing structure and routine in both family and personal daily life can provide a sense of predictability and stability. This is especially beneficial for navigating the unique aspects of parenting on the autism spectrum.

- **Practice Openness about Your Autism and Needs**

As much as possible, be open about your autism and your needs. Creating an environment of open communication fosters understanding and support, both within your family and your broader social circles.

While hiring help might not be accessible to everyone, for those who have the resources, it can be a valuable tool in managing the demands of parenting. The key is to recognize that seeking assistance is not a sign of weakness but a practical solution to ensure the well-being of both the parent and the child. It's about creating a support system that aligns with your unique needs and circumstances, fostering an environment where parenting becomes more manageable and enjoyable.

Key Takeaways

- Autistic individuals make exceptional parents, as they have unique strengths in parenting.
- Sensory challenges can be managed by creating sensory-friendly spaces.

- Autistic parents possess deep empathy, connecting with their children on a profound level.
- Embracing identity is crucial for self-acceptance and building a strong family dynamic.
- Managing shame involves self-compassion and seeking support from understanding individuals.
- Building a support network, including professional services and fellow parents, is essential.
- Prioritizing self-care and establishing routines help manage the demands of parenting.

In summary, embracing one's identity as an autistic parent, seeking support, and prioritizing self-care are vital for navigating the joys and challenges of parenting.

Conclusion

"Children with autism are colorful – they are often very beautiful, and, like the rainbow, they stand out." – Adele Devine.

Autism has a bad reputation and is often regarded as the big bad wolf that will destroy children. Many parents dread hearing the words "Your child is autistic," thinking that their child is doomed to a life of limitation. However, autism isn't a disease, and your child isn't sick; their brain just works differently. It is a disorder that can be managed with the proper management and lifestyle changes. This book provides you with all the information you need to give your child the life they deserve.

The book starts by introducing autism, its challenges, and the myths associated with this disorder. You also learned about the significance of early intervention and seeking help to get your child diagnosed and start management right away.

Autism impacts children's ability to feel empathy. You discovered how to reinforce this skill in your child, making them compassionate and understanding individuals. You also learned how to teach your child language skills so they can become more articulate.

Children with autism, like all children, want to be loved and accepted. You discovered how to celebrate your child's unique qualities and celebrate them for being special.

Your child's comfort begins at home. You discovered how to create a structured and comfortable environment for them to blossom and grow. You also learned the significance of establishing routines and rituals to eliminate surprises and create a stress-free home for them.

Some children with autism struggle with speaking and forming sentences. You discovered how to connect with your child through nonverbal communication. You learned how to read nonverbal cues and engage in nonverbal play to connect with them.

You then moved on to the most significant part of the book, the management. You learned how to customize a management plan for your child based on their strengths and needs. You understood the necessity of collaborating with care teams to work together for your child's benefit. You also explored different autism management options and therapies to find the best remedies for your child.

Children with autism's parents often neglect their own needs and only focus on their children. You discovered the power of self-care and having a support system to help you through tough times.

You learned how to advocate for your child's rights to ensure their needs are met and that they are accepted and treated as equals. The last chapter focused on autistic parents and how to use this advantage to help their children.

Let this book be your guide on your journey with your child. Apply everything you have learned and in time you will see a difference in your child.

References

5 Tips for Creating a Safe Home for Your Child with Autism. (2017, August 15). Www.appliedbehavioranalysisedu.org. https://www.appliedbehavioranalysisedu.org/5-tips-for-creating-a-safe-home-for-your-autistic-child/

7 Autism Behavior and Communication Strategies | NU. (2021, September 23). National University. https://nu.edu/blog/7-autism-behavior-and-communication-strategies/

80 Autism Quotes to Inspire and Educate. (2023, October 11). Www.apexaba.com. https://www.apexaba.com/blog/autism-quotes

Adams, T. (2004, September 12). A Home for Mr Naipaul. The Observer. https://www.theguardian.com/books/2004/sep/12/fiction.vsnaipaul

Amy Tobik, B. A. (2015, July 16). Quotes about Autism. Autism Parenting Magazine. https://www.autismparentingmagazine.com/quotes-about-autism/

Anonymous. (2008, October 27). How Does the Special Education System Work in the United States? Colorín Colorado. https://www.colorincolorado.org/article/how-does-special-education-system-work-united-states

Anxiety: Autistic Children and Teenagers. (2023, April 17). Raising Children Network. https://raisingchildren.net.au/autism/health-wellbeing/mental-health/anxiety-asd#:~:text=But%20autistic%20children%20might%20also

Apex Aba Therapy. (2023, October 11). 80 Autism Quotes to Inspire and Educate. Www.apexaba.com. https://www.apexaba.com/blog/autism-quotes

Art Therapy for Autism | Pingree Center. (2020, June 10). The Carmen B. Pingree Autism Center of Learning. https://carmenbpingree.com/blog/art-therapy-activities-for-autism/

Autism Diagnosis for Children: a Guide. (n.d.). Raising Children Network. https://raisingchildren.net.au/autism/learning-about-autism/assessment-diagnosis/autism-diagnosis#:~:text=To%20get%20a%20diagnosis%2C%20health

Autism Speaks. (2013). Seven Ways to Help Your Child with Nonverbal Autism Speak | Autism Speaks. Autism Speaks. https://www.autismspeaks.org/expert-opinion/seven-ways-help-your-child-nonverbal-autism-speak

Autism, PDD-NOS & Asperger's Fact Sheets | Using Positive Reinforcement for Behavior Management of Children with Asperger's Syndrome or Autism. (n.d.). Www.autism-Help.org. https://www.autism-help.org/behavior-positive-reinforcement-autism.htm

Ballen, K., & Kurtzberg, J. (2021). Exploring New Therapies for Children with Autism: "Do Not Try. Stem Cells Translational Medicine, 10(6), 823–825. https://doi.org/10.1002/sctm.20-0548

Being a Parent on the Autism Spectrum. (2017). https://heller.brandeis.edu/parents-with-disabilities/pdfs/autism-parent-factsheet.pdf

Bennie, M. (2023, March 1). Supporting Autistic Children through Structured Play. Autism Awareness. https://autismawarenesscentre.com/supporting-autistic-children-through-structured-play/

Bond, A. (2014, March 12). Kids with Family Routines More Emotionally, Socially Advanced. Reuters. https://jp.reuters.com/article/us-kids-family-routine/kids-with-family-routines-more-emotionally-socially-advanced-idUKBREA2B1TM20140312/

Burgess, R. (2019, March 5). Understanding the Spectrum – a Comic Strip Explanation. The Art of Autism. https://the-art-of-autism.com/understanding-the-spectrum-a-comic-strip-explanation/

CDC. (2022, March 28). Signs and Symptoms of Autism Spectrum Disorders. Centers for Disease Control and Prevention. https://www.cdc.gov/ncbddd/autism/signs.html

Centers for Disease Control and Prevention. (2019). Treatment and Intervention Services for Autism Spectrum Disorder. Centers for Disease Control and Prevention. https://www.cdc.gov/ncbddd/autism/treatment.html

Cpst, L. R. (2023, October 20). Pivoting: Balancing Self-Care While Caring for Your Autistic Child. Blue ABA. https://blueabatherapy.com/autism/self-care-for-carers-of-autistic-children/

Currigan, S. (2020, October 12). How to Teach Empathy to Kids with Autism. Beaconschoolsupport.co.uk. https://beaconschoolsupport.co.uk/newsletters/how-to-teach-empathy-to-kids-with-autism

Development of the IEP. (n.d.). Www.pacer.org. https://www.pacer.org/parent/iep/guide-to-iep/development-of-iep.asp

DeWeerdt, S. (2017, May 16). The Unexpected Plus of Parenting with Autism. Spectrum | Autism Research News. https://www.spectrumnews.org/features/deep-dive/unexpected-plus-parenting-autism/

Ellison, K. (2023, December 10). Autism Spectrum Disorder Treatment Plan & Example | Free PDF Download. Www.carepatron.com. https://www.carepatron.com/templates/autism-spectrum-disorder-treatment-plans

Fulghum, D. (2016, December 23). Tips for Parenting a Child on the Autism Spectrum. WebMD; WebMD. https://www.webmd.com/brain/autism/parenting-child-with-autism

Goally. (2023, June 14). How to Communicate with a Nonverbal Autism Child. Goalie Apps for Kids. https://getgoally.com/blog/nonverbal-autism/

Goally. (2023, May 30). How to Create an Autism Daily Routine. Goally Apps for Kids. https://getgoally.com/blog/how-to-create-an-autism-daily-routine/

Goally. (2023, October 24). 20 Autism Quotes We Love. Goally Apps & Tablets for Kids. https://getgoally.com/blog/20-quotes-about-autism-that-we-love/#10-quotes-about-autism-for-kids

golden-user. (2022, June 2). Positive Reinforcement Autism. Golden Care. https://www.goldencaretherapy.com/positive-reinforcement-autism/#:~:text=Positive%20reinforcement%20is%20important%20because

Government of Canada. (2018). Signs and Symptoms of Autism Spectrum Disorder (ASD) - Canada.ca. Canada.ca. https://www.canada.ca/en/public-health/services/diseases/autism-spectrum-disorder-asd/signs-symptoms-autism-spectrum-disorder-asd.html

Gray, C. (2015). What Is a Social Story? Carol Gray - Social Stories. https://carolgraysocialstories.com/social-stories/what-is-it/

Harris, N. (2023, July 16). Early Signs of Autism in Babies. Parents. https://www.parents.com/baby/health/autism/early-signs-of-autism-in-babies/

Hewitson, J. (2018, March 24). The Secret to… Raising a Happy Autistic Child. The Guardian; The Guardian. https://www.theguardian.com/lifeandstyle/2018/mar/24/the-secret-to-raising-happy-autistic-child

How to Communicate with a Nonverbal Autistic Child | The FCA. (n.d.). Www.thefca.co.uk. https://www.thefca.co.uk/fostering-autistic-children/communicating-with-a-nonverbal-child/

Kavanagh, C. (2023, March 29). Creating a Supportive Home Environment for Children with Autism. Autism Assessment Centre. https://autismassessmentcentre.ie/creating-a-supportive-home-environment-for-children-with-autism/

Kennedy Krieger Institute. (2013). Myths & Facts about Autism Spectrum Disorder. Kennedy Krieger.org;

Kennedy Krieger Institute. https://www.kennedykrieger.org/stories/myths-facts-about-autism-spectrum-disorder

Kesherim, R. (2023, November 9). 8 Types of Therapy for Autism to Consider. Www.totalcareaba.com. https://www.totalcareaba.com/autism/types-of-therapy-for-autism

LeBlanc, L. A., Esch, J., Sidener, T. M., & Firth, A. M. (2006). Behavioral Language Interventions for Children with Autism: Comparing Applied Verbal Behavior and Naturalistic Teaching Approaches. The Analysis of Verbal Behavior, 22(1), 49–60. https://www.ncbi.nlm.nih.gov/pmc/articles/PMC2774588/

Lee, C. I. (2022, August 9). The Strengths and Struggles of Being an Autistic Parent. LA Concierge Psychologist. https://laconciergepsychologist.com/blog/strengths-struggles-autistic-parent/

MColeman. (2021, April 6). 30 Quotes from 30 People with Autism. Els for Autism. https://elsforautism.org/30-quotes-from-30-people-with-autism/

Melinda. (2019, February 13). Autism Spectrum Disorders. HelpGuide.org. https://www.helpguide.org/articles/autism-learning-disabilities/autism-spectrum-disorders.htm

NHS. (2022, November 11). Signs of Autism in Children. NHS. https://www.nhs.uk/conditions/autism/signs/children/

Novak, S. (2022, December 2). Autism Myths and Facts. WebMD.

https://www.webmd.com/brain/autism/features/autism-myths-facts

Nummenmaa, L., Glerean, E., Hari, R., & Hietanen, J. K. (2013). Bodily Maps of Emotions. Proceedings of the National Academy of Sciences, 111(2), 646–651. https://doi.org/10.1073/pnas.1321664111

Nuñez, A. (2020, July 28). Turning Your Child's Interests into Passion. Autism Parenting Magazine. https://autismparentingmagazine.com/autism-child-passion/#:~:text=The%20beautiful%20thing%20about%20autism

Parents Guide to Autism. (2023, May 2). Child Mind Institute. https://childmind.org/guide/parents-guide-to-autism/

Petersson-Bloom, L., & Holmqvist, M. (2022). Strategies in Supporting Inclusive Education for Autistic Students—A systematic review of qualitative research results. Autism & Developmental Language Impairments, 7(1), 239694152211234. https://doi.org/10.1177/23969415221123429

Philadelphia, T. C. H. of. (2017, June 9). Evidence-Based Treatment Options for Autism. Www.chop.edu. https://www.chop.edu/news/evidence-based-treatment-options-autism

Raising Children Network. (2015, December 15). Language Development: Children with ASD. Raising Children Network. https://raisingchildren.net.au/autism/development/language-development/language-development-asd

Reid, S. (2023, October 11). Autism Treatments, Therapies, and Interventions - HelpGuide.org.

Https://Www.helpguide.org. https://www.helpguide.org/articles/autism-learning-disabilities/autism-treatments-therapies-interventions.htm

Rudy, L. J. (2023, November 13). Good Reasons Why Your Autistic Child Has a Tough Time With School. Verywell Health. https://www.verywellhealth.com/why-school-is-so-challenging-4000048

Schiller, J. (2023, February 27). Can Autistic People Have Kids? Thetreetop.com; The Treetop ABA Therapy. https://www.thetreetop.com/aba-therapy/can-autistic-people-have-kids

Schrandt, J. A., Townsend, D. B., & Poulson, C. L. (2009). Teaching Empathy Skills to Children with Autism. Journal of Applied Behavior Analysis, 42(1), 17–32. https://doi.org/10.1901/jaba.2009.42-17

Seeley, A. (2019, October 20). Taking Care of Yourself Benefits Your Loved One with Autism. Autism Society of NC; Autism Society of North Carolina. https://www.autismsociety-nc.org/taking-care-yourself/

Smith, M., Segal, J., & Hutman, T. (2019, March 20). Helping Your Child with Autism Thrive. HelpGuide.org. https://www.helpguide.org/articles/autism-learning-disabilities/helping-your-child-with-autism-thrive.htm

Team Stamurai. (2022, August 8). 9 Ways to Help Nonverbal Child with Autism Communicate. Stamurai.com. https://stamurai.com/blog/ways-to-help-nonverbal-child-with-autism-speak/

Therapies and Supports for Older Autistic Children and Teenagers. (n.d.). Raising Children Network. https://raisingchildren.net.au/autism/therapies-services/therapies-interventions/interventions-for-older-children-with-asd

Therapies for Parents and Carers. (n.d.). Com.au. https://www.autismawareness.com.au/therapies/parents-carers

Therapy, W. P. A. (2023, April 10). Coping Strategies for Parents and Caregivers of Children on the Autism Spectrum. WPA. https://www.wpatherapy.com/post/coping-strategies-for-parents-and-caregivers-of-children-on-the-autism-spectrum

TLC, B. (2021, January 5). 5 Ways to Help Your Child with Autism Show Empathy. Behavior TLC. https://behaviortlc.com/blog/help-your-child-with-autism-show-empathy/

TLC, B. (2022, May 1). Teaching Empathy Skills to Children with Autism: How to Help Them Understand and Cope with Social Situations. Behavior TLC. https://behaviortlc.com/blog/teaching-empathy-skills-to-children-with-autism/#:~:text=Help%20them%20label%20the%20emotions

Types of Therapy for Autism: 8 Therapies to Consider | Autism Resources. (2022, February 22). Www.songbirdcare.com. https://www.songbirdcare.com/articles/types-of-therapy-for-autism

Understanding Autism | Autism Awareness Australia. (2021). Www.autismawareness.com.au. https://www.autismawareness.com.au/understanding-autism

Upham, B., & Mackenzie, S. (n.d.). Self-Care for Autism Caregivers. Everydayhealth.com. https://www.everydayhealth.com/autism/how-to-care-for-yourself-when-you-re-caring-for-someone-with-autism/

Verywell Health. (2019). Where and How Should My Autistic Child Go to School? Verywell Health. https://www.verywellhealth.com/educational-options-for-children-with-autism-260393

Vrana, C. (n.d.). Leveraging Special Interests to Help Children with Autism: An Autistic Person* Shares Her Experiences. Blog.stageslearning.com. https://blog.stageslearning.com/blog/leveraging-special-interests-to-help-children-with-autism-an-autistic-person-shares-her-experiences

White, J., McGarry, S., Falkmer, M., Scott, M., Williams, P. J., & Black, M. H. (2023). Creating Inclusive Schools for Autistic Students: A Scoping Review on Elements Contributing to Strengths-Based Approaches. Education Sciences, 13(7), 709. https://doi.org/10.3390/educsci13070709

Yi, L., Pan, J., Fan, Y., Zou, X., Wang, X., & Lee, K. (2013). Children with Autism Spectrum Disorder Are More Trusting Than Typically Developing Children. Journal of Experimental Child Psychology, 116(3), 755–761. https://doi.org/10.1016/j.jecp.2013.05.005

Yost Abrams, K. (n.d.). Communication Tools for Nonverbal Autistic Children. Www.jigsaw-Dx.com. https://www.jigsaw-dx.com/post/communication-tools-for-nonverbal-autistic-children

Your Child's Rights: Autism and School. (n.d.). Autism Speaks. https://www.autismspeaks.org/autism-school-your-childs-rights#:~:text=IDEA%20specifies%20that%20children%20with

Your Rights in School: A Good Education for All - Autistic Self Advocacy Network. (2020, June 25). Https://Autisticadvocacy.org/. https://autisticadvocacy.org/actioncenter/issues/school/

Printed in Great Britain
by Amazon